BASIC TRAINING

A BELIEVER'S GUIDE TO SPIRITUAL BATTLE

by

Kim Freeman

Harrison House
Tulsa, Oklahoma

06 05 04 03   10 9 8 7 6 5 4 3 2 1

Basic Training—
A Believer's Guide to Spiritual Battle
ISBN 1-57794-575-1
Copyright © 2003 by Kim Freeman
P.O. Box 1668
St. Peters, MO 63376
kfreeman@cotr.org

Published by Harrison House, Inc.
P.O. Box 35035
Tulsa, Oklahoma 74153

Contents

Dedication

To Patsy Cameneti, one of my earliest mentors in the faith. Your initial interest in this project has been a continual source of inspiration. Your teaching and example have impacted my life more than you will ever know.

PREFACE

Regardless of how the media may try to spin it, the events of September 11, 2001, thrust the world into a spiritual war of epic proportions. What's happening on the world scene now is not really about politics or economics. It's about darkness versus light, evil versus good. (See Eph. 6:12.)

Unless we understand that, we're going to end up wasting precious time, energy, and resources on solutions destined to fail. That's not to say there aren't steps we have to take in the natural realm. But unless those steps are ordered by the Lord, we're going to find ourselves fearful, worried, frustrated, and confused. In the worst-case scenario, we might even find ourselves fighting against God through disobedience or misunderstanding His will.

Most books on spiritual warfare focus on the subject of prayer, and rightly so. Prayer is a vital component of spiritual warfare, and I encourage all believers to learn as much as they can about it so they can develop and grow in that area.

But prayer is not the only component. In fact, if we focus on prayer to the exclusion of the other elements of spiritual warfare, we're going to come up short.

The underlying theme of this book is that spiritual warfare isn't an event, it's a lifestyle. It's not just something we do at church or at special prayer meetings; it's something we live—twenty-four hours a day, seven days a week.

We're at a very critical point in history now. Many believe that these are the last days.[1] The pace is picking up, spiritually speaking. Right before our eyes events are clicking off on God's prophetic timetable more rapidly than ever before.

We don't have time to be caught up in worldly things anymore. We don't have time to play church anymore. It is very likely that the Lord will be returning soon. People's eternal destinies are at stake. Every moment counts now. Everything is strategic now.

It's time to get in step with God, for our own sake as well as for the sake of other people. It is my prayer that the truths contained in the following pages will help us to do that. Glory to God!

KIM FREEMAN

INTRODUCTION
THE ARMY OF GOD

In his letter to the Philippians, the apostle Paul makes a statement that reveals the multifaceted nature of the Church.

> Yet I supposed it necessary to send to you Epaphroditus, my brother, and companion in labour, and fellowsoldier....
>
> Philippians 2:25

Although we often speak of belonging to the family of God once we are born again, Paul makes it clear that the Church is more than just a family. It's more than just a charitable social organization. It's an army.

One dictionary tells us that an army is "a large organized body of armed personnel trained for war...."[1] It also defines an army as "a body of persons organized to advance a cause."

Notice again some of the characteristics that define an army: organization, weapons, training, and a cause.

Let's look at the Word of God and see if we find these characteristics in the Church.

IS THE CHURCH ORGANIZED?

Yes, we see that in the letters of Paul when he describes the Church as the body of Christ, with Jesus Himself as the Head.

...Christ is the head of the church, his body, of which he is the Savior.

Ephesians 5:23 NIV

And he is the head of the body, the church....

Colossians 1:18

The body is a unit, though it is made up of many parts; and though all its parts are many, they form one body. So it is with Christ.

Now the body is not made up of one part but of many.

But in fact God has arranged the parts in the body, every one of them, just as he wanted them to be.

1 Corinthians 12:12,14,18 NIV

Although it's true that men throughout history have tried to make the Church conform to their own plans and designs, the true Church has always taken her pattern and instructions from the Lord.

DOES THE CHURCH HAVE WEAPONS?

Yes, again, we read about them in the letters of Paul.

> For though we walk (live) in the flesh, we are not carrying on our warfare according to the flesh and using mere human weapons.
>
> For the weapons of our warfare are not physical (weapons of flesh and blood), but they are mighty before God for the overthrow and destruction of strongholds.
>
> 2 Corinthians 10:3,4 AMP

> For our struggle is not against flesh and blood, but against the rulers, against the authorities, against the powers of this dark world and against the spiritual forces of evil in the heavenly realms.
>
> Therefore put on the full armor of God, so that when the day of evil comes, you may be able to stand your ground, and after you have done everything, to stand.

Stand firm then, with the belt of truth buckled around your waist, with the breastplate of righteousness in place,

And with your feet fitted with the readiness that comes from the gospel of peace.

In addition to all this, take up the shield of faith, with which you can extinguish all the flaming arrows of the evil one.

Take the helmet of salvation and the sword of the Spirit, which is the word of God.

And pray in the Spirit on all occasions with all kinds of prayers and requests. With this in mind, be alert and always keep on praying for all the saints.

Ephesians 6:12-18 NIV

The Church is not a natural army using natural weapons in a natural war. This isn't about bombs and guns and tanks. The Church is a spiritual army using spiritual weapons in a spiritual war. It's about truth and righteousness and the souls of men.

DOES THE CHURCH RECEIVE TRAINING IN WARFARE?

Yes, and from the best Trainer possible—Lord Sabaoth!

This particular name of God, Sabaoth, is usually translated "the Lord of hosts" and is used to identify Him as the One who is supreme ruler over all the (spiritual) armies of heaven.[2] So even though it is clear from the Scriptures that God is a God of love to His people, it is also clear that He is a God of war against evil.

> The Lord is a warrior....
>
> Exodus 15:3 NIV

> Blessed be the Lord, my Rock and my keen and firm Strength, Who teaches my hands to war and my fingers to fight.
>
> Psalm 144:1 AMP

Not only do we have God's armor and weapons at our disposal, we have His wisdom and expertise to guide us and direct us and prepare us for battle against the forces of darkness.

DOES THE CHURCH
HAVE A CAUSE?

The answer to that question is a definite yes! Our cause is the Gospel of Jesus Christ.

Fight the good fight of faith; lay hold of the eternal life to which you were summoned and [for which] you confessed the good confession [of faith] before many witnesses.

1 Timothy 6:12 AMP

...I am sending you—

To open their eyes that they may turn from darkness to light and from the power of Satan to God, so that they may thus receive forgiveness and release from their sins and a place and portion among those who are consecrated and purified by faith in Me.

Acts 26:17,18 AMP

Our cause in this warfare is to walk in the light ourselves and to carry that light to others.

Organization, weapons, training, and a cause—the Church has all the components that define an army. God has given us everything we need to be able to function effectively in this capacity. The only question now is, will we?

A HEAVENLY SUMMONS

There's a stirring going on in the earth today. God is issuing a summons.

> Listen, a noise on the mountains, like that of a great multitude! Listen, an uproar among the kingdoms, like nations massing together! The Lord Almighty is mustering an army for war.
>
> Isaiah 13:4 NIV

God is stirring His people to rise up and take their place in His army in these last days. Time is short. He has plans that must be carried out. He has purposes that must be fulfilled. And we are the ones He has chosen to fulfill them.

In times past, it may have been possible for believers to lag behind and avoid the heat of battle. Those days are over. J.M. Spaight, who was principal secretary of Britain's Air Ministry, spoke prophetically when he addressed the British House of Commons in World War II: "It is a commonplace that today we are all in the front line. The era of absenteeism in war-waging is dead and gone."[3]

The heat is on. We're in God's army now, like it or not. We're on the front line now, like it or not.

This isn't the time to be halfhearted. This isn't the time to be a casual Christian. This is the time to follow God with all our heart and mind and soul and strength. If we don't, we're going to be picked off by the enemy.

In the early days of the Church, Paul exhorted Timothy to be a first-class soldier and to shoulder his share of responsibility for furthering the kingdom of God.

> Take [with me] your share of the hardships and suffering [which you are called to endure] as a good (first-class) soldier of Christ Jesus.
>
> 2 Timothy 2:3 AMP

Timothy and the early saints heeded those words. Should we do any less today?

PRINCIPLE #1

CUT OFF THE
ENEMY'S SUPPLY LINES

[Grant] understood that...supplies, crops, stock, as well as arms and ammunition—everything that was necessary in order to carry on the war, was a weapon in the hands of the enemy; and of every weapon the enemy must be deprived.[1]

—RUSSELL F. WEIGLEY
History of the United States Army

To strike at the army, you struck at the economy that supported it. It was then a slightly new theory as far as formal warfare was concerned, but today is embodied in the bombing raids all countries carry out in an effort to destroy factories, railroad lines, warehouses, anything that the opposing economy needs.[2]

—BRUCE CATTON
Reflections on the Civil War

PRINCIPLE #1

Cut Off the Enemy's Supply Lines

Author William Seymour makes an insightful observation in his book *Decisive Factors in Twenty Great Battles of the World* that I believe will help us in our study of how to become first-class soldiers in the army of God.

Tactics...[due to changes in weapons over the centuries], and the science of war will change with the times, but the underlying principles remain constant and were as vital in battles fought in ancient days as those fought in the twentieth century.[3]

In other words, there are certain principles regarding warfare that are true for all times. We ignore them at our peril.

If we want to be successful in our warfare against the devil, if we want to walk in victory and help others do the same, then we'll need to learn these principles and follow them.

STAY OUT OF SIN

The first principle we want to look at is that of cutting off the enemy's supply lines. The goal here is to eliminate the enemy's resources for making and carrying on war as much as possible.

We see an example of this in the Word of God when Sennacherib, King of Assyria, invaded Judah. Notice King Hezekiah's response as Sennacherib approached Jerusalem.

> When Hezekiah saw that Sennacherib had come and that he intended to make war on Jerusalem,
>
> he consulted with his officials and military staff about blocking off the water from the springs outside the city, and they helped him.
>
> A large force of men assembled, and they blocked all the springs and the stream that flowed through the land. "Why should the kings of Assyria come and find plenty of water?" they said.
>
> Then he worked hard repairing all the broken sections of the wall and building towers on it. He built another wall outside that one and reinforced the supporting terraces of the City of David....
>
> 2 Chronicles 32:2-5 NIV

When Hezekiah found out that the enemy was approaching, he immediately looked for those vulnerable areas which Sennacherib might be able to exploit (in this case, fresh water and broken-down walls) and made the appropriate adjustments.

In a natural war, vulnerable areas could include all kinds of things, such as food, water, utilities, transportation, and communication. But in the spiritual war in which we are engaged, one of the things that makes us most vulnerable to our enemy is sin.

Sin separates us from God; in that sense, it cuts us off from His power. The reason is that God is holy, and He cannot dwell with unholiness.[4]

Moses warned the Israelites about this very thing as they were getting ready to enter the Promised Land.

> When you go forth against your enemies and are in camp, you shall keep yourselves from every evil thing.
>
> For the Lord your God walks in the midst of your camp to deliver you and to give up your enemies before you. Therefore shall your camp be holy, that He may see nothing indecent among you and turn away [or retreat] from you.
>
> Deuteronomy 23:9,14 AMP

If we want to have God's power and Presence manifested through us, both individually and corporately, then we have to live pure and holy lives.[5] That kind of life comes from studying and meditating on the Word, and then walking it out on a daily basis with God's help.

Does that mean we'll never sin?

No, we're all in the process of learning to keep our flesh under the control of our spirit. But it does mean that we need to be quick to repent when we fail and do wrong.

Harboring sin in our life is an open invitation to the devil. It gives him permission to step in and do whatever he wants to do in our circumstances. And until we repent of that sin, we're powerless to resist him.

Remember the story of Achan in the Old Testament? It's a perfect illustration of the danger of playing with sin.

In that story, God had just given the Israelites a stunning, dramatic victory over the city of Jericho. (See Josh. 6:20.) Because this was the first city the Israelites conquered in the Promised Land, God wanted them to set it apart as a kind of first-fruits offering. They were not to keep any of the spoil for themselves. The items of silver, gold, bronze, and iron that they had captured were to be put into the treasury of the Lord, and everything else in the city was to be destroyed. (See Josh. 6:18,19.)

But one man, Achan, couldn't resist the temptation. He took a few things for himself and hid them in his

tent. (See Josh. 7:1.) Because he experienced no imme-
diate judgment for his actions, Achan probably believed
his sin had gone unnoticed—by God and everyone
else—and that he was "safe." As we will see, the rest of
the story proves otherwise.

After the Jericho victory, Joshua sent some men to
spy out another nearby city, Ai. Because it was discov-
ered that Ai was much smaller and less intimidating
than Jericho, Joshua decided that it wasn't necessary to
send the entire Israelite army; a few thousand men
would be able to handle it.

So off they went. But they were totally unprepared
for what happened next.

> So about three thousand men went up; but they
> were routed by the men of Ai,
>
> who killed about thirty-six of them. They chased
> the Israelites from the city gate as far as the stone
> quarries and struck them down on the slopes. At this
> the hearts of the people melted and became like water.
>
> Then Joshua tore his clothes and fell facedown to
> the ground before the ark of the Lord, remaining
> there till evening. The elders of Israel did the same,
> and sprinkled dust on their heads.
>
> And Joshua said, "Ah, Sovereign Lord, why did
> you ever bring this people across the Jordan to deliver

us into the hands of the Amorites to destroy us? If only we had been content to stay on the other side of the Jordan!

O Lord, what can I say, now that Israel has been routed by its enemies?

The Canaanites and the other people of the country will hear about this and they will surround us and wipe out our name from the earth. What then will you do for your own great name?"

The Lord said to Joshua, "Stand up! What are you doing down on your face?

Israel has sinned; they have violated my covenant, which I commanded them to keep. They have taken some of the devoted things; they have stolen, they have lied, they have put them with their own possessions.

That is why the Israelites cannot stand against their enemies; they turn their backs and run because they have been made liable to destruction. I will not be with you anymore unless you destroy whatever among you is devoted to destruction.

Go, consecrate the people. Tell them, 'Consecrate yourselves in preparation for tomorrow; for this is what the Lord, the God of Israel, says: That which is devoted is among you, O Israel. You cannot stand against your enemies until you remove it.'"

Joshua 7:4-13 NIV

As the story goes on, it becomes evident that Achan is the culprit. As a result, he, his family, and his possessions were destroyed. After the sin had been purged from the camp, God once again accompanied the Israelites into battle, and they were able to take the city of Ai, as He originally intended.

The message is pretty clear here. Harboring sin in our life makes it impossible for us to stand against the enemy.

Let's go back for a few moments and look at some parts of the story a little more closely.

First of all, we see that Achan wasn't the only person affected by his sin. Thirty-six innocent men lost their lives in the initial battle with Ai, and the Word of God lays the blame squarely at the feet of Achan.

But the destruction doesn't stop there. The consequences of Achan's sin eventually spread to include his entire family. (See vv. 24-26.)

The statement "It's my life; what I do with it doesn't matter, as long as I don't hurt anyone else" is the watchword of our culture. People say that kind of thing all the time. The only problem is that unless you live on a remote desert island somewhere and never have contact with another human being, the chances of your sin never affecting anyone else are nil (even if that were possible, your sin would still be an affront to God).

The Bible tells us that the way we live influences others, whether we like it or not.

> He who heeds instruction and correction is [not only himself] in the way of life, but is a way of life for others. And he who neglects or refuses reproof [not only himself] goes astray, [but also] causes to err and is a path toward ruin for others.
>
> Proverbs 10:17 AMP

So the real question is not, "*Will* my life affect other people?" The question is, "*How* will my life affect other people?"

Obviously, it's better for us, and everyone around us, when we obey God.

Notice something else in Joshua 7:7. God is the first one to be blamed for the problem.

Isn't that so like human nature? So quick to blame somebody else for our problems—especially God—and so slow to examine our own lives or take any responsibility for our own behavior.

Proverbs 19:3 NIV sums it up nicely:

A man's own folly ruins his life, yet his heart rages against the Lord.

That tendency started with Adam and has continued ever since. (See Gen. 3:11,12.) Unfortunately, it will keep us enslaved to sin if we don't learn to be honest with ourselves and face up to the truth.

The truth is that God is never our problem; He is our Answer. He tells us to stay out of sin because it will ruin us, not because He's down on "fun." And even when we sin, there is forgiveness and restoration available to us through the shed blood of Jesus, if we'll humble ourselves and turn to Him. (See 1 John 1:9.)

We need to understand one thing, though. When sin is the problem, nothing will fix it but repentance. Praying won't fix it. Fasting won't fix it. Giving special offerings won't fix it. Yelling at the devil won't fix it. Getting every ministry on television to agree with us in prayer won't fix it. Only repentance will fix it.

After the Ai defeat, we see Joshua on his face, crying out to God about how bad things are. And what happens? God basically tells him he's wasting his time!

Joshua didn't need to cry and whine or fast and pray for a week. Now fasting and praying are essential elements of our relationship with God, but neither those things nor crying and whining were going to impress God or change one thing about Joshua's situation.

The problem was sin. Joshua just needed to find out where it was and get rid of it.

We see a similar kind of statement in the book of Isaiah.

> Behold, the Lord's hand is not shortened at all, that it cannot save, nor His ear dull with deafness, that it cannot hear.
>
> But your iniquities have made a separation between you and your God, and your sins have hidden His face from you, so that He will not hear.
>
> Isaiah 59:1,2 AMP

It's not that God has grown weary after all these years of running the universe. It's not that He wins some and loses some now that He's older. It's not that He's become a little hard of hearing and just doesn't pick up on our prayers quite like He used to. He's not the problem; we are.

If we're harboring sin in our life, we—not God, not the devil, not other people—have obstructed the flow of God's power and blessing to us. And the plain truth is that it's not going to get any better *until* we get rid of that sin.

THE EXCEPTION, NOT THE RULE

Look again at Joshua 7:12. God didn't say, "I will not be with you anymore." He said, "I will not be with you anymore *unless* you destroy whatever among you is devoted to destruction."

It's not that God *wants* to break fellowship with us when we sin. He *has* to; light can't fellowship with darkness. (See 2 Cor. 6:14.) But He's eager to resume fellowship with us as soon as we get back into right relationship with Him. We do that by repenting.

Repenting is not just feeling sorry for our sin. We can do that without repenting. Repenting is turning around and going in the opposite direction. In other words, we stop sinning and start obeying God.

Don't misunderstand. The Bible makes it clear in Ephesians 2:8-9 that we are saved by grace, not by works. We don't earn our salvation through obedience. Only the blood of Jesus can atone for our sins and put us in right standing with God. But that doesn't mean obedience isn't important.

Obedience is the evidence that our salvation is genuine. Yes, we're still going to make mistakes, and God has made provision for that. First John 1:9 tells us that when we confess our sins, He is faithful and just to forgive us and cleanse us from all unrighteousness.

What a blessing! We just need to make sure we don't allow that blessing to become an excuse for continuing in a sinful lifestyle, as both Paul and Peter warn us against doing.

> Well then, shall we keep on sinning so that God can keep on showing us more and more kindness and forgiveness?
>
> Of course not! Should we keep on sinning when we don't have to?
>
> For sin's power over us was broken when we became Christians and were baptized to become a part of Jesus Christ; through his death the power of your sinful nature was shattered.
>
> Romans 6:1-3 TLB

> [Live] as free people, [yet] without employing your freedom as a pretext for wickedness; but [live at all times] as servants of God.
>
> 1 Peter 2:16 AMP

If we have grown comfortable with sin as a believer, something is wrong. That may have been the norm for us when we were in the world, but that's not our nature anymore. For us, sin should be the exception, not the rule.

BECOME UNTOUCHABLE

A number of years ago, there was a television program called "The Untouchables." It centered around the gangsters of the Capone era and the government agents who sought to bring them to justice.

The basis of the story was that although corruption was rampant in the law enforcement community at that time, one special group of government agents had come to be regarded as "The Untouchables." They were morally clean. They couldn't be bought. They couldn't be corrupted. There was nothing in them that gave their enemies access into their lives.

You could say that Jesus was that way, that He was untouchable. He even talked about it during some of the last moments He spent with His disciples.

> Hereafter I will not talk much with you: for the prince of this world cometh, and hath nothing in me.
>
> John 14:30

The Amplified Bible says it like this:

I will not talk with you much more, for the prince (evil genius, ruler) of the world is coming. And he has no claim on Me. [He has nothing in common with Me; there is nothing in Me that belongs to him, and he has no power over Me.]

Jesus never left an open door for the devil. He never allowed sin to have a place in His life. As a result, the devil had no authority over Him. The devil had no legal point of entry into His life.

Because of what Jesus accomplished by sacrificing Himself for us, the same can be said of every believer today—the devil has no authority over us.

Jesus plainly stated that fact in Luke 10:19 AMP:

Behold! I have given you authority and power to trample upon serpents and scorpions, and [physical and mental strength and ability] over all the power that the enemy [possesses]; and nothing shall in any way harm you.

Because of the grace of God, we can exercise the same authority over the devil that Jesus did. That's a spiritual reality.

The problem is that when we sin, we give up that authority. When we sin, we open the door to the enemy, and in effect, give him permission to invade our lives.

We need to settle it in our hearts once and for all that sin is like a magnet to the devil. It gives him something in common with us. It attracts him to us and gives him legitimate access into our lives. And as long as we harbor that sin and keep playing around with it, we won't be able to exercise any real authority over him. The reason is, our sin gives him a legal right to be there. In fact, we could even say that he's there at our invitation.

I have heard that after the Watergate scandal, someone asked former President Richard Nixon how it felt to be stabbed in the back by his enemies. He regretfully admitted that he had given them the knife. Whenever we play around with sin, we make the same mistake.

Before we start whining and complaining about how we're being attacked by the devil, we may need to check up on ourselves a little bit. As we saw earlier with Hezekiah, maybe we need to take a look around and see if there is anything in our life that is leaving us vulnerable to the enemy.

Have we left a door open for him somewhere? Have we given him the knife, so to speak? If so, then it's time to cut off his supply lines. It's time to make some adjustments. It's time to start living the kind of life that will enable us to say, "The devil has nothing in me."

PRINCIPLE #2

STAY IN TOUCH WITH HEADQUARTERS

Thomas spared no pains, an aide said, to see that his army was 'well supplied, well looked after, and always brought to the right place at the right time.'[1]

—DAVID NEVIN
Sherman's March: Atlanta to the Sea

Good or bad intelligence can have a decisive effect on the outcome of a battle.[2]

—WILLIAM SEYMOUR
*Decisive Factors in Twenty
Great Battles of the World*

In the Battle of Brandywine, Washington did not exercise good intelligence supervision, failed to distinguish true from false information and relied too much on subordinates.[3]

—NORTH CALLAHAN
George Washington: Soldier and Man

PRINCIPLE

STAY IN TOUCH
WITH HEADQUARTERS

#2

We just finished talking about the importance of cutting off the enemy's supply lines. But there's a flip side to that. We have to be sure to keep our own supply lines open.

Countless battles in history have been lost because armies failed to sustain a steady flow of support (such as communication, food, and supplies) from their headquarters. Countless spiritual battles have been lost for the same reason.

The Bible makes it clear that maintaining an intimate relationship with God (by talking to Him and reading the Word daily) is crucial to our success and effectiveness in life.

> Dwell in Me, and I will dwell in you. [Live in Me, and I will live in you.] Just as no branch can bear fruit of itself without abiding in (being vitally united to)

the vine, neither can you bear fruit unless you abide in Me.

I am the Vine; you are the branches. Whoever lives in Me and I in him bears much (abundant) fruit.

However, apart from Me [cut off from vital union with Me] you can do nothing.

John 15:4,5 AMP

In other words, what Jesus appears to be saying is that apart from a personal relationship with God, life is basically a waste of time and effort.

VITALLY UNITED

John 15:4-5 is not talking about just any old kind of relationship. Jesus says we need to be "vitally united" to Him. What does He mean? Let's look at a few more verses.

You have said, Seek My face [inquire for and require My presence as your vital need]. My heart says to You, Your face (Your presence), Lord, will I seek, inquire for, and require [of necessity and on the authority of Your Word].

Psalm 27:8 AMP

Seek, inquire of and for the Lord, and crave Him and His strength (His might and inflexibility to temptation); seek and require His face and His presence [continually] evermore.

Psalm 105:4 AMP

If we're vitally united to Him, we understand that all we are and all we have comes from God. If we're vitally united to Him, we understand that to be separated from Him is to be separated from the very Source of Life. If we're vitally united to Him, we cling to Him in the same way that we cling to our next breath.

Actually, we just read a word in Psalm 105:4 that sums up the idea of being vitally united quite well—*crave.*

Did you ever *really* crave something? It's almost unbearable. Suddenly, satisfying that desire becomes the focal point of your life. You'll rearrange your priorities, change your plans, get up in the middle of the night, go anywhere, do anything, and make any sacrifice to satisfy that craving.

Do we crave God like that? Is our desire for fellowship with Him so intense that it's almost unbearable to us? Is satisfying that desire for Him the focal point of our life?

If not, then we still haven't quite arrived at the point of being vitally united to Him.

Part of the problem is that we haven't really learned what it means to abide in Him.

The word *dwell* that we saw in John 15:4 (or abide as stated in the *King James Version*) literally means "to stay (in a given place, state, relation or expectancy)."[4] You could say it means to live as a resident.

But that's not quite how some Christians define dwell. To them, *dwell* means "to check in once in awhile" (on Sundays, for example). To them, *dwell* means "to talk to God when I need something; otherwise, I've got things to do, places to go, and people to see." Their relationship with God is all about convenience, not commitment.

God is not interested in that kind of relationship. He has so much more for us than a relationship of convenience will allow. So many things He wants to share with us. So many things He wants to give to us. But they can't be conveyed in what amounts to a drive—through devotion or a microwaved moment with Him. That's why He is looking for hearts that are given over to Him completely. He's looking for hearts that desire and crave His Presence "continually evermore."

The Jews have a special word for this kind of devotion: *d'vekut*. It literally means "cleaving to the Shekinah" (Divine Presence), and they believe it is the ultimate goal of life.

To cleave is to stick to like glue,[5] and we see something of that meaning in the word *d'vekut*. In his book *Jewish Spiritual Practices*, author Yitzhak Buxbaum describes *d'vekut* as "the intensification of love of God until that love is so strong that you cleave to Him without separation."[6] He goes on to quote another source as saying that *d'vekut* is "the most intense love, such that you are not separated from God for even a moment."[7]

That's what Jesus had in mind when He talked about being vitally united to Him. He wants us to stick to Him like glue. He wants us to be consumed with Him. He wants our thoughts, our words, and our deeds to be so centered around Him and His purposes that we're never separated from Him—not even for a moment.

COME CLOSER

God wants us to be vitally united to Him. But that won't happen just because He wants it. It will only happen if *we* want it.

Let's go back for a moment and look once again at the first few words of John 15:4 AMP:

Dwell in Me, and I will dwell in you....

As we see in this verse, our dwelling in God comes first; then His dwelling in us comes about as a result of that. If we think it's going to be any other way, we are mistaken.

Moses found that out. Remember his encounter with God at the burning bush?

> Now Moses kept the flock of Jethro his father-in-law, the priest of Midian; and he led the flock to the back or westside of the wilderness, and came to Horeb or Sinai, the mountain of God.
>
> The Angel of the Lord appeared to him in a flame of fire out of the midst of a bush; and he looked, and behold, the bush burned with fire, yet was not consumed.
>
> And Moses said, I will now turn aside and see this great sight, why the bush is not burned.
>
> And when the Lord saw that he turned aside to see, God called to him out of the midst of the bush and said, Moses, Moses! And he said, Here am I.
>
> Exodus 3:1-4 AMP

This encounter ushered Moses into a level of relationship with God that he had not experienced up until that time, a relationship that eventually enabled him to actually speak with God "face to face" (Ex. 33:11).

But Moses had to choose it.

True, God made the initial effort to get Moses' attention. But that was as far as God could go in Moses' life until Moses responded to Him.

Look at the passage again. It says that God spoke to Moses "...when the Lord saw that he turned aside to see..." (v. 4).

When Moses took the time and initiative to come closer to God, God came closer to him.

The Word tells us that God draws us with His loving-kindness:

> "I have loved you with an everlasting love; I have drawn you with loving-kindness."
>
> Jeremiah 31:3 NIV

God desires with all His heart to have an intimate, personal relationship with us. But He is not a dictator. He's a Gentleman. So instead of overpowering us and forcing us to come to Him, He woos us and courts us with His love. The rest is up to us.

We don't have to wonder about the heart of God. The Word is very clear about His intentions.

> Come near to God and he will come near to you
> ... purify your hearts, you double-minded.
>
> James 4:8 NIV

Notice it doesn't say that He *might* come closer if we come closer. It says that He *will*. He's already made up His mind about us. As we see in the second part of that verse, the problem is that we haven't made up our mind about Him.

In his book *Enjoying Intimacy With God*, J. Oswald Sanders makes this provocative statement:

> *We are now, and will be in the future, only as intimate with God as we really choose to be.*[8]

As *we* choose to be—don't miss that.

We already have access to intimacy with God through the finished work of His Son Jesus. That's God's standing invitation to us.

> For it is through Him that we both [whether far off or near] now have an introduction (access) by one (Holy) Spirit to the Father [so that we are able to approach Him].
>
> Ephesians 2:18 AMP

> In Whom, because of our faith in Him, we dare to have the boldness (courage and confidence) of free

access (an unreserved approach to God with freedom
and without fear).

Ephesians 3:12 AMP

The only question now is, what are we going to do
with that invitation?

These passages tell us that God's invitation gives us
access to Him. But access is simply the *freedom* to
approach Him and develop a relationship with Him.
The degree to which we *exercise* that freedom is up to us.

In his devotional classic *My Utmost for His Highest,*
Oswald Chambers warns, "...Beware of stopping short
of abandonment to God...."[9]

The word *abandon* means "to give up to the control
or influence of another person...."[10] Are we there yet
with God? Are we willing to give ourselves up completely to His control and influence?

If we want our lives to be fruitful and productive for
the Lord, then we're going to have to abandon ourselves
to Him completely—no holding back, no looking back,
no turning back.

Abraham was like that. He was totally abandoned to
God and His will.

Some time later God tested Abraham. He said to him, "Abraham!" "Here I am," he replied.

Then God said, "Take your son, your only son, Isaac, whom you love, and go to the region of Moriah. Sacrifice him there as a burnt offering on one of the mountains I will tell you about."

Early the next morning Abraham got up and saddled his donkey. He took with him two of his servants and his son Isaac. When he had cut enough wood for the burnt offering, he set out for the place God had told him about.

On the third day Abraham looked up and saw the place in the distance.

He said to his servants, "Stay here with the donkey while I and the boy go over there. We will worship and then we will come back to you."

When they reached the place God had told him about, Abraham built an altar there and arranged the wood on it. He bound his son Isaac and laid him on the altar, on top of the wood.

Then he reached out his hand and took the knife to slay his son.

But the angel of the Lord called out to him from heaven, "Abraham! Abraham!" "Here I am," he replied.

"Do not lay a hand on the boy," he said. "Do not do anything to him. Now I know that you fear God,

because you have not withheld from me your son,
your only son."

Genesis 22:1-5,9-12 NIV

In this case the commandment of God ran totally
contrary to common sense and Abraham's natural
mind. But it didn't matter. He had abandoned himself
to God. He didn't hold back; he didn't look back; he
didn't turn back. Whatever God wanted from Abraham,
He could have.

God is looking for that same kind of heart in His
people today. To see the real issue, all we have to do is
take a closer look at His last statement in verse 12:

"...Now I know that you fear God, because you
have not withheld from me...."

Genesis 22:12 NIV

God is looking for people who will not withhold
from Him—in their thoughts, in their devotion, in their
time, in their finances, in their possessions, in their
service, in their relationships—people who will not
withhold *anything* He asks of them.

God is looking for people who will say to Him,
"Father, all that I have and all that I am are Yours."

When He finds them, He will say to them, "And, My child, all that I have and all that I am are yours."

Intimacy with God is our choice. The more we give ourselves to Him, the more He gives Himself to us. As far as He's concerned, there's no limit.

We already know what God wants. Now it's time for us to decide what we want.

WONDERFUL COUNSELOR

How does all of this relate to spiritual warfare and being in the army of God?

One of the benefits we receive when we abandon ourselves to Him is His counsel. And the Bible tells us that in warfare, sound counsel is a must.

> Purposes and plans are established by counsel;
> and [only] with good advice make or carry on war.
> Proverbs 20:18 AMP

> For by wise counsel you can wage your war, and in
> an abundance of counselors there is victory and safety.
> Proverbs 24:6 AMP

Spiritual warfare is serious business. The stakes are high. We had better know what we're doing.

If we're not in touch with God, we're going to be lost on the battlefield. Without His wisdom and direction, we'll be easy prey for the enemy.

We must not misunderstand the passage in Proverbs 24:6 about having an abundance of counselors. That doesn't mean we need to run around and ask everybody else what they think we should do every time we're faced with a difficult situation.

The Word of God interprets itself on this issue:

> Your testimonies also are my delight and my counselors.
>
> Psalm 119:24 AMP

God's Word (His "testimonies") is our "abundance of counselors." He has all the wisdom we need. True, He may choose to *confirm* His Word to us through other people, but we *must* stay in the habit of going to Him directly first as our Source of wisdom.

Isaiah 9:6 AMP refers to God as the "Wonderful Counselor." The word *wonderful* means "...marvelous... unusually good."[11] The word *marvelous* means "causing amazement or admiration; miraculous; supernatural; of the highest kind or quality; notably superior."[12] And as if that weren't enough, Proverbs 21:30 NIV drives the point home even further:

> There is no wisdom, no insight, no plan that can succeed against the Lord.

Wow! Why would we even think about looking anywhere else for direction? Anything or anyone else would be second best. If we'll just stick with God, if we'll just stay in touch with our spiritual headquarters, our victory is certain. Remember, we do that by spending time talking to God and staying filled with His Word.

Unfortunately, too many Christians spend more time talking with other Christians than they spend talking with God. Worse yet, some even turn to godless men and women in the world for advice.

God actually calls that rebellion, which indicates disobedience and opposition to authority,[13] and He has some rather strong things to say about it in His Word:

> Woe to the rebellious children, says the Lord, who take counsel and carry out a plan, but not Mine, and who make a league and pour out a drink offering, but not of My Spirit, thus adding sin to sin;
>
> Who set out to go down into Egypt, and have not asked Me—to flee to the stronghold of Pharaoh and

to strengthen themselves in his strength and to trust in the shadow of Egypt!

Therefore shall the strength and protection of Pharaoh turn to your shame, and the refuge in the shadow of Egypt be to your humiliation and confusion.

Yet will all be ashamed because of a people [the Egyptians] who cannot profit them, who are not a help or benefit, but a shame and disgrace.

For Egypt's help is worthless and toward no purpose....

Isaiah 30:1-3,5,7 AMP

Sounds serious, doesn't it? If we want to keep from being disgraced and defeated on the battlefield, we need to take these words to heart.

Let's look closer at this passage for just a moment, starting with the very first word: *woe.*

What, exactly, is meant by the word *woe?* One dictionary defines it as "a condition of deep suffering from misfortune, affliction, or grief; ruinous trouble; calamity," or "inconsolable grief or misery."[14]

That certainly doesn't sound very good. But God says that is what we can expect if we follow any other plan for our life but His.

Are we saying that these things are some kind of punishment that God holds in store for people who cross Him?

No, woe is just the natural consequence of following second best, our own counsel instead of His.

In this passage, Egypt and Pharaoh represent types of the world. Notice the words that describe what we will experience if we follow them—shame, humiliation, confusion, and disgrace.

Who needs any of that?

Note, too, that verse five doesn't just say that the world's wisdom *might* not profit us. It says that it *cannot* profit us. As far as spiritual matters are concerned, the world's help is worthless.

If we're following the wisdom of the world or our own understanding, we're in trouble.

> ...it is not in man [even in a strong man or in a man at his best] to direct his [own] steps.
>
> Jeremiah 10:23 AMP

None of us is really capable of ordering our own lives. We need the counsel of God.

God already understands that. He just wants to make sure that we do.

When God tells us to obey His Word, it's not because He has an ego problem and just enjoys bossing people around. He's trying to spare us the inevitable pain and suffering that result when we go our own way.

God loves us. He's for us. He made that clear from the very beginning, when He first delivered His Word to us.

> The Lord commanded us to obey all these decrees and to fear the Lord our God, so that we might always prosper and be kept alive, as is the case today.
>
> Deuteronomy 6:24 NIV

Don't miss this! Almighty God, King of the universe, is on *our* side, and He wants us to be *thoroughly* blessed in every area of our life! We don't need to try to discover another pathway to victory. This is it. If we'll stay vitally united to Him and follow His counsel, we'll always come out on top.

PRINCIPLE #3

KNOW YOUR ENEMY

One draws a clear dividing line between one's self and the enemy. His word is not to be believed; the enemy who means well does not exist....[1]

—EAST GERMAN COLONEL LANGER,
cited by Martin Ebon
The Soviet Propaganda Machine

"[He] doesn't make a bad enemy," [General Eichelberger] said shortly after landing in Subic Bay, "as we can always expect the worst of him and govern ourselves accordingly...."[2]

—GENERAL EICHELBERGER,
cited by Francis Trevelyan Miller
History of World War II

Few battles, if any, were ever won by the total elimination of the losing force...a rapid undermining of the morale of an army is often more efficacious than the simple infliction of casualties.[3]

—CHARLES GRANT
Wargame Tactics

We shall break down the enemy psychologically before the armies begin to function...mental confusion...indecision... panic...these are our first weapons.[4]

ADOLF HITLER,
cited by Francis Trevelyan Miller
History of World War II

PRINCIPLE

KNOW YOUR ENEMY

#3

One thing we can definitely say about the devil is that he makes a "good" devil. He's bad to the core, and he's consistent about it. We can always expect the worst from him.

But there's something else we can say about him: he's a loser—past, present, and future.

> You were blameless in your ways from the day you were created until iniquity and guilt were found in you.
> Through the abundance of your commerce
> you were filled with lawlessness and violence, and you sinned; therefore I cast you out as a profane thing from the mountain of God....
>
> Ezekiel 28:15,16 AMP

[God] disarmed the principalities and powers that were ranged against us and made a bold display and

41

public example of them, in triumphing over them in Him and in it [the cross].

Colossians 2:15 AMP

Behold! I have given you authority and power to trample upon serpents and scorpions, and [physical and mental strength and ability] over all the power that the enemy [possesses]; and nothing shall in any way harm you.

Luke 10:19 AMP

Then the devil who had led them astray [deceiving and seducing them] was hurled into the fiery lake of burning brimstone, where the beast and false prophet were; and they will be tormented day and night forever and ever (through the ages of the ages).

Revelation 20:10 AMP

As we see in these Scriptures, the devil's a mess. He's a failure. He's defeated. He's doomed to destruction. So why do we seem to have so much trouble with him?

The reason is ignorance. We haven't really understood the truth about him and how he operates.

The fact is that we've been a little out of balance in this area. World-renowned author C.S. Lewis stated it correctly in his preface to *The Screwtape Letters:*

There are two equal and opposite errors into which our race can fall about the devils. One is to disbelieve in their existence. The other is to believe, and to feel an excessive and unhealthy interest in them.[5]

We don't want to make the mistake of looking for a demon under every rock and in every nook and cranny. But we don't want to be naive, either.

Let's set the record straight about a few things right up front. The devil is not the equal opposite of God. God doesn't have any equals—good, bad, or otherwise. Nobody compares to Him. And although the devil *opposes* God, he is not truly the *opposite* of God. As a created being—a fallen angel, to be exact—he is really more the opposite of Michael the archangel.[6]

God is often described as omnipotent, omnipresent, and omniscient. The prefix *omni-* means "all...."[7] With that in mind, we could say that *omnipotent* means He's "all-powerful," *omnipresent* means He's "present in all places at all times," and *omniscient* means He's "all-knowing."[8]

The devil, on the other hand, isn't *omni-* anything. He's certainly no match for God.

Just look at how the Word describes the conflict with God that ended in Satan's departure from heaven:

And He said to them, I saw Satan falling like a lightning [flash] from heaven.[9]

Luke 10:18 AMP

And the huge dragon was cast down and out— that age-old serpent, who is called the Devil and Satan, he who is the seducer (deceiver) of all humanity the world over; he was forced out and down to the earth, and his angels were flung out along with him.

Revelation 12:9 AMP

The expressions "falling like a lightning [flash]" and "flung out" do not seem to refer to a being of superior power and majesty. In fact, one of the definitions of *fling* is "to place or send suddenly and unceremoniously...."[10] Make no mistake about it. This wasn't some long, drawn-out affair between evenly matched foes. It was all over in an instant. The devil never knew what hit him.

As a result, Satan and his evil cohorts now have a very healthy fear of God.

You believe that God is one; you do well. So do the demons believe and shudder [in terror and horror such as make a man's hair stand on end and contract the surface of his skin]!

James 2:19 AMP

They've had a taste of God's wrath firsthand. They don't have to wonder about it.

We might have guessed that the devil would be afraid of God. But something we haven't really understood is that he's also afraid of us.

Let's look for a moment at an eye-opening account of Saul and David in 1 Samuel 18. Keep in mind that in this passage, Saul is a type of the devil, and David is a type of the believer.

> Saul was afraid of David, because the Lord was with him but had departed from Saul.
>
> When Saul saw how capable and successful David was, he stood in awe of him.
>
> When Saul saw and knew that the Lord was with David and that Michal [his] daughter loved him,
>
> Saul was still more afraid of David; and Saul became David's constant enemy.
>
> 1 Samuel 18:12,15,28,29 AMP

Why is the devil our constant enemy?

Look again at what the Word says in this passage. He's afraid of us. He knows God is *with* us and *in* us. And as long as that's the case, we're a threat to the devil and his demonic kingdom.

45

Our position is far greater than we realize. Paul tells us in his letter to the Ephesians that because of what Jesus accomplished on the cross, we are *already* seated in a place of victory with Him.

And [so that you can know and understand] what is the immeasurable and unlimited and surpassing greatness of His power in and for us who believe, as demonstrated in the working of His mighty strength,

Which He exerted in Christ when He raised Him from the dead and seated Him at His [own] right hand in the heavenly [places],

Far above all rule and authority and power and dominion and every name that is named [above every title that can be conferred], not only in this age and in this world, but also in the age and the world which are to come.

And He has put all things under His feet....

Paul goes on to say in Chapter 2:

And He raised us up together with Him and made us sit down together [giving us joint seating with Him] in the heavenly sphere [by virtue of our being] in Christ Jesus (the Messiah, the Anointed One).

Ephesians 1:19-22; 2:6 AMP

Notice that the word *raised* is past tense. In other words, it's over. It's finished.

We're *already* seated in a place of victory with Jesus, *far* above *all* rule and authority and power—and *all* includes the devil.

If that's the case, then how is he going to stop us? Besides the passage we just looked at, didn't we read earlier in Colossians 2:15 that God has disarmed him? Then how can he possibly defeat us? The only way is through deception. It's the only thing he has left.

He has to trick us into believing *his* words (which come to us as negative thoughts or negative comments made by others) instead of God's Word. It may not sound like much, but he's had years and years of practice, and he's very good at it. It would be a mistake to underestimate him.

LIAR! LIAR!

The Bible specifically tells us to be aware of how the devil operates.

> Lest Satan should get an advantage of us: for we are not ignorant of his devices.
>
> 2 Corinthians 2:11

We need to know our enemy. This is classic war strategy. If we don't, this verse says that he will gain an advantage over us.

Think about that for a moment. If he has to *gain* the advantage, then that must mean he doesn't already have it.

That lines right up with another familiar Bible passage:

> Be sober, be vigilant; because your adversary the devil, as a roaring lion, walketh about, seeking whom he may devour.
>
> 1 Peter 5:8

"May" is the key word in this verse. It means to "...have permission to...."[11] In other words, the devil has an advantage over us only when we give it to him. We do that by believing his lies instead of the truth.

The Bible plainly tells us that God is the Source of truth and that knowing His truth makes us free.

> ...Your Word is Truth.
>
> John 17:17 AMP

> And you will know the Truth, and the Truth will set you free.
>
> John 8:32 AMP

Following God's Word leads to victory and triumph. The devil, however, is the source of falsehood. If we fall for his lies, we're headed for bondage.

> ...He was a murderer from the beginning and does not stand in the truth, because there is no truth in him. When he speaks a falsehood, he speaks what is natural to him, for he is a liar [himself] and the father of lies and of all that is false.
>
> John 8:44 AMP

Following the devil's words leads to oppression and defeat.

The first few verses of Psalm 10 talk about "the wicked one." We can look at this person as a type of the devil.

Verse 7 is particularly revealing:

> His mouth is full of cursing, deceit, oppression (fraud)....

Cursing, deceit, oppression, and fraud are really all the devil knows. His mouth is full of them.

If we look at these words a little more closely, we'll gain some insight into the devil's strategy.

To *curse* is "to use profanely insolent language against."[12]

To *deceive* is "to cause to accept as true or valid what is false or invalid...." It "implies...imposing a false idea or belief that causes ignorance, bewilderment, or helplessness...."[13]

To *oppress* is "...to crush or burden by abuse of power or authority...to burden spiritually or mentally: weigh heavily upon."[14]

Fraud is the "...intentional perversion of truth in order to induce another to part with something of value or to surrender a legal right...."[15]

The military has a word for this kind of strategy: *disinformation*. It is defined as "false information deliberately and often covertly spread...in order to influence public opinion or obscure the truth."[16]

That's exactly what the devil's up to: spreading false information and obscuring the truth. He's going to do anything and everything he can to try to get us to doubt the Word of God.

So, now we know what we can expect from the devil. But we must also understand that he doesn't do it just once in awhile or just on Monday mornings or just at home or just at work. He does it everywhere, all the time.

STAND FAST

There are a lot of things we could say about the devil and his strategies. We could go through the entire Bible, find passage after passage, piece them all together, and come up with a very detailed picture of how he operates.

For the sake of time, however, we're going to focus on three specific passages that summarize the devil's tactics probably better than any other portions of the Word of God. One is in 2 Chronicles and the other two are in Nehemiah.

Let's start with the passage in 2 Chronicles. In this case, Sennacherib (king of Assyria) represents a type of the devil.

> After these things and this loyalty, Sennacherib king of Assyria came, invaded Judah, and encamped against the fortified cities, thinking to take them....
>
> And this Sennacherib king of Assyria, while he himself with all his forces was before Lachish, sent his servants to Jerusalem, to Hezekiah king of Judah, and to all Judah who were at Jerusalem, saying,
>
> Thus says Sennacherib king of Assyria: On what do you trust, that you remain in the strongholds in Jerusalem?

Is not Hezekiah leading you on in order to let you die by famine and thirst, saying, The Lord our God will deliver us out of the hand of the king of Assyria?

Has not the same Hezekiah taken away His high places and His altars, and commanded Judah and Jerusalem, You shall worship before one altar and burn incense upon it?

Do you not know what I and my fathers have done to all the people of other lands? Were the gods of the nations of those lands in any way able to deliver their lands out of my hand?

Who among all the gods of those nations that my fathers utterly destroyed was able to deliver his people out of my hand, that your God should be able to deliver you out of my hand?

So now, do not let Hezekiah deceive or mislead you in this way, and do not believe him, for no god of any nation or kingdom was able to deliver his people out of my hand or the hand of my fathers. How much less will your God deliver you out of my hand!

And his servants said still more against the Lord God and against His servant Hezekiah.

The Assyrian king also wrote letters insulting the Lord, the God of Israel, and speaking against Him, saying, As the gods of the nations of other lands have not delivered their people out of my hand, so shall not the God of Hezekiah deliver His people out of my hand.

And they shouted it loudly in the Jewish language to the people of Jerusalem who were on the wall, to frighten and terrify them, that they might take the city.

And they spoke of the God of Jerusalem as they spoke of the gods of the peoples of the earth, which are the work of the hands of men.

For this cause Hezekiah the king and the prophet Isaiah son of Amoz prayed and cried to heaven.

And the Lord sent an angel, who cut off all the mighty warriors and commanders and officers in the camp of the king of Assyria. So the Assyrian king returned with shamed face to his own land....

Thus the Lord saved Hezekiah and the inhabitants of Jerusalem from the hand of Sennacherib the king of Assyria and from the hand of all his enemies, and He guided them on every side.

2 Chronicles 32:1,9-22 AMP

Now let's go back and take a closer look at this story.

To begin with, it's important to notice that King Hezekiah and the people of Judah were already in a position of strength. Verse 1 refers to the cities as "fortified" and verse 10 tells us that Jerusalem was a "stronghold." And although the cities did have certain natural fortifications, the real key to the people's strength was that God was on their side.

Sennacherib already knew that. That's why he spent the next nine verses trying to convince them otherwise. He knew that the only way he could win was to get the people to doubt God and to doubt their place of security in Him.

Isn't that just like the devil? Compare the taunts in verses 11 through 15 with these updated versions (author's paraphrases):

"God's not going to help you. He's forgotten about you. He's mad at you. You've probably committed the unpardonable sin.

"Besides that, Sister so-and-so had this very same problem and things didn't work out too well for her. In fact, I don't know anybody who's ever gotten out of a situation this bad. It's hopeless! God couldn't help you even if He wanted to. You might as well give up!"

Sound familiar?

On top of that, he hammers it over and over and over again through as many different avenues as possible. His goal is to wear us down with continual pressure so that we eventually cave in and surrender to him.

We can see this pattern clearly illustrated in the story we just read. Verse 16 tells us that Sennacherib's servants said "still more." Verse 17 says that he "also wrote letters" with the same basic message. Verse 18 describes how his servants "shouted it loudly in the Jewish language." All of this was designed to simply wear the people down.

Make no mistake about it. The devil is going to be loud, in your face, day after day, with a message tailor-made for you. That's just the way he is. That's just his style.

That doesn't mean we need to panic. It just means we need to be prepared.

Near the end of this passage, we find a major key to handling the devil's attacks. Notice in verse 18 that Sennacherib's purpose was "...to frighten and terrify them, that they might take the city." The clear implication is that unless Sennacherib *could* frighten and terrify them, he *couldn't* take the city!

What would frighten or terrify them most?

The idea that God couldn't—or wouldn't—help them. So that's exactly the area Sennacherib zeroed in on.

According to verse 19, his servants "...spoke of the God of Jerusalem, as they spoke of the gods of the people of the earth...." He wanted the people to see their God as weak, helpless, indifferent, and unresponsive.

The good news for the people of God then and now is that our God is not like other gods. He's mighty! He's awesome! He loves us! He's ready to move on our behalf! All we have to do is believe Him and rely on Him, and He'll deliver us and guide us on every side.

Hezekiah reminded the people about that right up front.

> Be strong and courageous. Be not afraid or dismayed before the king of Assyria and all the horde that is with him, for there is Another with us greater than [all those] with him.
>
> With him is an arm of flesh, but with us is the Lord our God to help us and to fight our battles. And the people relied on the words of Hezekiah king of Judah.
>
> 2 Chronicles 32:7,8 AMP

Hezekiah let the people know that no matter how bad it looked or how bad it sounded, they didn't have to be afraid of the enemy. There was "Another" with them.

What a truth! There is Another with us!

No matter what the devil brings our way, there is Another with us, greater than anything and everything he can come up with! All we have to do is stand fast in the Lord our God and on His Word.

Consider this: If Sennacherib had the ability to overthrow the people of God, why didn't he just storm in and do it? Why waste all that time mouthing off and playing mind games?

It's obvious that he had to have the people's cooperation. *He couldn't take the city unless they gave it to him.*

The devil is the same way. He needs our cooperation in order to be able to make any headway in our life. He has to have our permission.

If the devil really had the ability to stop us on his own, he would have prevented us from being born again. Why would he want to allow us to become indwelt by the very Spirit of God Himself? Talk about a tactical blunder!

The truth is that he *can't* stop us. When we make the determination to stand fast on the Word of God and see it through to fulfillment, there's ultimately *nothing* the devil can do about it.

That's not to say he isn't going to try, but the Bible gives us the remedy for that.

> Submit yourselves therefore to God. Resist the
> devil, and he will flee from you.
>
> James 4:7

This verse tells us that we are to submit (yield) to God in everything, but we must never submit (yield) to the devil in anything. When we courageously and boldly oppose the enemy, he flees.[17] The word *flee* means "...to hurry toward a place of security."[18] He won't like it, and he probably won't go quietly, but he'll go. The devil knows he's not safe around the Word of God.

Notice it says "will flee," not might flee. If we'll stand firm against him, the devil *must* go. He'll be the one who has to return with shamed face to his own land. He doesn't have a choice.

STAY FOCUSED

The two other passages we want to look at on this are found in Nehemiah. Here, Sanballat and his cohorts are also types of the devil. Let's keep an eye open for spiritual parallels as we read.

> When Sanballat heard that we were rebuilding
> the wall, he became angry and was greatly incensed.
> He ridiculed the Jews,

and in the presence of his associates and the army of Samaria, he said, "What are those feeble Jews doing? Will they restore their wall? Will they offer sacrifices? Will they finish in a day? Can they bring the stones back to life from those heaps of rubble—burned as they are?"

Tobiah the Ammonite, who was at his side, said, "What they are building—if even a fox climbed up on it, he would break down their wall of stones!"

Hear us, O our God, for we are despised. Turn their insults back on their own heads. Give them over as plunder in a land of captivity.

Do not cover up their guilt or blot out their sins from your sight, for they have thrown insults in the face of the builders.

So we rebuilt the wall till all of it reached half its height, for the people worked with all their heart.

But when Sanballat, Tobiah, the Arabs, the Ammonites and the men of Ashdod heard that the repairs to Jerusalem's walls had gone ahead and that the gaps were being closed, they were very angry.

They all plotted together to come and fight against Jerusalem and stir up trouble against it.

But we prayed to our God and posted a guard day and night to meet this threat.

Meanwhile, the people in Judah said, "The strength of the laborers is giving out, and there is so much rubble that we cannot rebuild the wall."

Also our enemies said, "Before they know it or see us, we will be right there among them and will kill them and put an end to the work."

Then the Jews who lived near them came and told us ten times over, "Wherever you turn, they will attack us."

Therefore I stationed some of the people behind the lowest points of the wall at the exposed places, posting them by families, with their swords, spears and bows.

After I looked things over, I stood up and said to the nobles, the officials and the rest of the people, "Don't be afraid of them. Remember the Lord, who is great and awesome, and fight for your brothers, your sons and your daughters, your wives and your homes."

When our enemies heard that we were aware of their plot and that God had frustrated it, we all returned to the wall, each to his own work.

From that day on, half of my men did the work, while the other half were equipped with spears, shields, bows and armor. The officers posted themselves behind all the people of Judah who were building the wall. Those who carried materials did their work with one hand and held a weapon in the other,

and each of the builders wore his sword at his side as he worked....

Neither I nor my brothers nor my men nor the guards with me took off our clothes; each had his weapon, even when he went for water.

Nehemiah 4:1-18,23 NIV

Now let's look at Nehemiah 6:1-9,15,16 NIV.

When word came to Sanballat, Tobiah, Geshem the Arab and the rest of our enemies that I had rebuilt the wall and not a gap was left in it—though up to that time I had not set the door in the gates—

Sanballat and Geshem sent me this message: "Come, let us meet together in one of the villages on the plain of Ono." But they were scheming to harm me;

so I sent messengers to them with this reply: "I am carrying on a great project and cannot go down. Why should the work stop while I leave it and go down to you?"

Four times they sent me the same message, and each time I gave them the same answer.

Then, the fifth time, Sanballat sent his aide to me with the same message, and in his hand was an unsealed letter in which was written: "It is reported among the nations—and Geshem says it is true—that you and the Jews are plotting to revolt, and therefore you are building the wall. Moreover, according to these reports you are about to become their king

and have even appointed prophets to make this proclamation about you in Jerusalem: 'There is a king in Judah!' Now this report will get back to the king; so come, let us confer together."

I sent him this reply: "Nothing like what you are saying is happening; you are just making it up out of your head."

They were all trying to frighten us, thinking, "Their hands will get too weak for the work, and it will not be completed." [But I prayed,] "Now strengthen my hands."

So the wall was completed on the twenty-fifth of Elul, in fifty-two days.

When all our enemies heard about this, all the surrounding nations were afraid and lost their self-confidence, because they realized that this work had been done with the help of our God.

Here we find another very interesting story. Although the spiritual parallels are more numerous than we can cover in the scope of this chapter, we do want to highlight a few of them.

As in 2 Chronicles 32, we see that the devil's tactics haven't changed. His pattern is one of nonstop provocation, ridicule, insults, harassment, pressure, and threats, both night and day, day and night.

What's intriguing is that Nehemiah, like Hezekiah, really doesn't give the enemy that much attention. For the most part, they both simply stay alert, keep their focus on God, pray, and do their best to follow whatever instructions He gives them. In fact, Nehemiah doesn't even address the enemy until after two entire chapters. And even then, he makes it short and sweet—the equivalent of "Go away! I'm busy!"

Actually, that's not a bad principle to follow. If we find ourselves spending all our time rebuking the devil and taking our cues from him, it's a pretty clear indication that we've gotten off track.

We will never bear much fruit as Christians unless we stay focused. If the devil can't get us involved in blatant sin, he'll try to see to it that we become preoccupied with all kinds of distractions and the cares of this life. We've been duped by that trick for generations. If we want to be productive, we're going to have to stop falling for it.

We have to remember our God-given assignment—to build the kingdom of God, not ferret out devils. If the devil gets in our way, we can nail him with the Word, but then we've got to go right back to building. If we don't, we're going to lose ground. We're going to be walking out the devil's agenda instead of God's.

We have to learn how to be offensive as well as defensive. Remember how Nehemiah described the people? He said they "did their work with one hand and held a weapon in the other" (Neh. 4:17).

That's the way we have to be. We already know that the devil is going to show up on a regular basis and that God has provided us with the spiritual equipment to be able to handle him when he does. But we're not supposed to just be sitting around waiting for him. We've got a job to do!

It's important to remember, too, that the devil is a liar. Most of the things he tries to intimidate us with aren't even real. Nehemiah was right when he said, "Nothing like what you are saying is happening; you are just making it up out of your head" (Neh. 6:8).

Think about it. After all of the mouthing off by the enemy in the previous passages, nothing happened in either story. Not one thing that the enemy said to them came to pass—not one.

There's a lesson for us here. Most of the things we worry about never even come to pass. The devil's bluffing. He doesn't have what it takes to pull things off, as long as we stand our ground.

The Bible has a word for the devil's taunts and threats and harassment: *noise.*

> [And I am distracted] at the noise of the enemy....
>
> Psalm 55:3 AMP

The dictionary defines "noise" as "loud, confused, or senseless shouting...any sound that is undesired or interferes with one's hearing of something...irrelevant or meaningless data or input [bits or words] occurring along with desired information..." and "...something that attracts attention...."[19]

I'd say that's a very good description of the devil's chatter.

If the devil is anything, he's noisy. All for the sole purpose of drawing our attention away from God and His Word. We can count on that.

We can't listen to lies and walk in liberty. We have to stay alert. We have to be discerning. We have to stay focused. Our victory depends on it.

TIMING IS EVERYTHING

One final thing we can say about the devil: If there's anything he understands, it's timing.

We find one of the clearest statements of this principle in Luke 4, where we read about Jesus being tempted by the devil in the wilderness.

Then Jesus, full of and controlled by the Holy Spirit, returned from the Jordan and was led in (by) the [Holy] Spirit

For (during) forty days in the wilderness (desert), where He was tempted (tried, tested exceedingly) by the devil. And He ate nothing during those days, and when they were completed, He was hungry.

Then the devil said to Him, If You are the Son of God, order this stone to turn into a loaf [of bread].

And Jesus replied to him, It is written, Man shall not live and be sustained by (on) bread alone but by every word and expression of God.

Then the devil took Him up to a high mountain and showed Him all the kingdoms of the habitable world in a moment of time [in the twinkling of an eye].

And he said to Him, To You I will give all this power and authority and their glory, (all their magnificence, excellence, preeminence, dignity and grace,) for it has been turned over to me, and I give it to whom I will.

Therefore if You will do homage to and worship me [just once], it shall all be Yours.

And Jesus replied to him, Get behind Me, Satan! It is written, You shall do homage to and worship the Lord your God, and Him only shall you serve.

Then he took Him to Jerusalem, and set Him on a gable of the temple, and said to Him, If You are the Son of God, cast Yourself down from here;

For it is written, He will give His angels charge of you to guard and watch over you closely and carefully;

And on their hands they will bear you up, lest you strike your foot against a stone.

And Jesus replied to him, [The Scripture] says, You shall not tempt (try, test exceedingly) the Lord your God.

And when the devil had ended every [the complete cycle of] temptation, he [temporarily] left Him [that is, stood off from Him] until another more opportune and favorable time.

Then Jesus went back full of and under the power of the [Holy] Spirit into Galilee....

Luke 4:1-14 AMP

This is such a familiar passage to us that we sometimes gloss over it. But there are some things here we must be careful not to miss.

Look back at verse 13 for a moment. Notice that it refers to the devil's series of temptations as "the complete cycle." In other words, he has a limited arsenal. It's true that he may try to repackage things to suit our particular situation, but it's the same old stuff he's been using on everyone since the Garden of Eden. (See Gen. 3:1-5.) It all boils down to questioning the Word of God in one way or another.

But his key to making it all work is timing. Notice Luke 4:13 goes on to say that he backed off from Jesus temporarily to wait for a "more opportune and favorable time." As we know, with Jesus, he never found such a time. But with us, it's an entirely different story.

The fact is that we're not always on top of things. So the devil will wait. He'll wait until we're tired. He'll wait until the washing machine goes out. He'll wait until our spouse makes a sarcastic remark. He'll wait until we've had to spend two hours in traffic due to an accident, which ended up making us miss a key appointment. He'll wait until we've had to spend the entire day with four screaming kids and a disgruntled mother-in-law.

He'll wait until we've missed three days in a row of spending any kind of quality time with God. He'll wait—and he'll win—if we don't handle those opportunities the way Jesus did.

Does that mean screaming at the devil until we hyperventilate?

No, it means staying full of the Spirit and answering every temptation with the Word of God.

Notice in verses 1 and 14 that Jesus went *into* the situation full of the Spirit, and He *left* full of the Spirit. The truth is, He just lived that way all the time. That was His key to victory. And the more we walk (live)[20] in the Spirit, the more *we* will walk in victory as well.

Fortunately, the devil's not the only one who understands timing. If we'll follow God's leading, we'll find ourselves in the right place at the right time with the right words for any and every circumstance we face.

We see from this passage that Jesus used the Word of God to counter every attack of the enemy. But it wasn't a hit-or-miss proposition. He didn't just rattle off every Scripture He could think of that had to do with those subjects and hope something hit the target. The Holy Spirit prompted Him in His heart with what to say and how to say it, and those words hit their mark exactly, perfectly.

We need to follow that pattern. Too many times we get all shook up emotionally when we're under attack. We start yelling at the devil—usually more out of fear than faith at that point—spouting off every verse we can think of, whether it applies or not. We look like somebody flailing away at a piñata. No wonder we don't get any results.

The devil isn't affected by volume; he isn't affected by a multitude of words. He's affected by the Word of God, spoken in faith under the inspiration, leading, and power of the Holy Spirit.

In Ephesians 6 Paul talks about our spiritual armor. Let's look at one of the pieces he mentions.

> ...and the sword of the Spirit, which is the word of God.

> Ephesians 6:17

The Amplified Bible says:

> ...and the sword that the Spirit wields, which is the Word of God.

If we look carefully at these two translations of this verse, we'll discover something that will help us use the Word more effectively against the enemy.

Some of us have missed it by thinking that the Word of God was *our* sword, so *we've* tried to wield it in our own power, ability, and inspiration. Consequently, we haven't always obtained the kind of results we want.

The expression *sword of the Spirit* doesn't just mean that the sword is spiritual in nature. It means that it's the Spirit's sword; it belongs to Him. He is the One who has to wield it if our blows to the enemy are going to make an impact.

The word *wield* means "to handle...effectively."[21] Who better to handle the Word of God effectively than the One who inspired it? (See 2 Tim. 3:16.)

Our job is simply to feed on the Word of God and plant it in our hearts. The Holy Spirit's job is to wield that sword by drawing the right words out of us at the right time. When that happens it will bring the most damage to the devil, the most glory to God, and the most blessing to us.

Our enemy doesn't have any defense against the Word of God or the Spirit of God. If we'll stay full of the Word and walk in the Spirit, the devil will have to go.

He'll have to wait for a more opportune time. And we can make sure he never finds one.

PRINCIPLE #4

KEEP RANK

...Whatever the task, the Commando forces had specialists trained for that job.[1]

—FRANCIS TREVELYAN MILLER

History of World War II

On the Ides of March the Allies unleashed an unheard-of fury against Cassino.... That destruction, ironically, owed much to a young man from East Orange, New Jersey, who had never actually fought in a battle. Captain David Ludlum, before the war, had taught history in a boarding school and amused himself with meteorology as a hobby; but in the army his hobby became his assignment. It was his long, painstaking study of his weather charts that determined the date and time for the gigantic bombardment....[2]

—FRANCIS TREVELYAN MILLER

History of World War II

In this endeavor [driving the Germans from Africa] the cooperation of land, sea, and air forces was superb. All functioned together as smoothly as if each were an integrated part of the same perfectly designed machine....[3]

—FRANCIS TREVELYAN MILLER

History of World War II

PRINCIPLE

KEEP RANK

#4

In his book *Wargame Tactics*, Charles Grant states:

...[in warfare], it is vital to make a correct choice of troops for a particular operation....[4]

It doesn't matter how much firepower is available, how great the field position, or how clever the strategy. Without the right people in the right place at the right time, victory is uncertain.

Nobody knows that better than God. That's why He hasn't left anything to chance. He has a perfect plan for carrying out His purposes in the earth, and each one of us has a particular assignment in that plan. It is not something determined by our parents or something just drawn out of a hat somewhere. It is something that we were specially and uniquely fashioned to do by God Himself.

That's not just true for preachers and other people in ministry; it's true for every one of us.

But as it is, God has placed and arranged the limbs and organs in the body, each [particular one] of them, just as He wished and saw fit and with the best adaptation.

Now you [collectively] are Christ's body and [individually] you are members of it, each part severally and distinct [each with his own place and function].

1 Corinthians 12:18,27 AMP

These two verses clearly indicate that *all* the parts of the body of Christ have a special assignment and that God is the One who made those assignments.

Notice in verse 18 that He has positioned us as *He* saw fit. He didn't bother to ask our opinion. He didn't take a poll of all our friends and family members to ask them what they thought about it. He already had a plan for us, and He created us to fit perfectly into that plan.

We learn something of God's pattern in this process in the book of Jeremiah.

Before I formed you in the womb I knew [and] approved of you [as My chosen instrument], and before you were born I separated and set you apart, consecrating you; [and] I appointed you as a prophet to the nations.

Jeremiah 1:5 AMP

Notice the sequence of events: He knew us, He set us apart for His purposes, He appointed us to a particular work, and *then* He formed us to be perfectly suited and equipped for that assignment.

God didn't have to wait until we showed up before He could decide what to do with us. He didn't have to give us an aptitude test to try to figure out where we might fit. He had already pictured us as being part of His plan before we were ever born. He had already decided where we fit and what He wanted us to do before we ever got here. And then He carefully shaped us and intricately fashioned us so that we showed up ready-made to function in that role.

In other words, we've been custom-built. We don't just happen to have certain gifts and abilities. We don't just happen to have certain dreams and desires in our heart. God made us that way on purpose so that we could carry out the special assignment He has given us.

He didn't just do this for a select few. He did it for all of us. He designed a special place for each one of us where we will fit and flow with those around us and supply something of eternal value to those whose lives we touch.

ETERNITY IN OUR HEART

If we're going to stay in step with God in this hour, we're going to have to hook up with His plans and purposes. We're going to have to develop an eternal perspective about life in general and about *our* life in particular.

That won't be as difficult as it sounds because God's already given us a head start on that.

> ...[God] also has planted eternity in men's hearts and minds [a divinely implanted sense of a purpose working through the ages which nothing under the sun but God alone can satisfy]....
>
> Ecclesiastes 3:11 AMP

> From one man He made every nation of men, that they should inhabit the whole earth; and He determined the times set for them and the exact places where they should live.
>
> God did this so that men would seek Him....
>
> Acts 17:26-27 NIV

God created us with a built-in hunger for Him and His purpose for our life that is intended to draw us to Him for further instruction. The plan is supposed to lead us to the Planner.

Unfortunately, we don't always pick up on that right away. We sense something pulling at our heart, but instead of letting it lead us to God, we try to satisfy that hunger with other things—entertainment, activities, hobbies, relationships, careers. But nothing quite hits the spot—not even ministry—unless it's connected to His eternal purpose for us.

Our heart will never be satisfied until we're fulfilling God's will for our life. Let's just settle that issue right now. It will save us a lot of time, money, and frustration and make us a lot more productive and effective for the kingdom of God.

We must not confuse being busy with being fruitful. It's easy to be busy. There are lots of things we *could* do. But unless we're doing the things we were specially created by God to do, we're wasting time.

We're not here by accident. We don't just happen to be alive at this time. We don't just happen to live where we live. We don't just happen to have a hunger in our heart. God's up to something! If we want to be fruitful, we'll discover what it is and get with the program.

"WHY AM I HERE?"

Designing our purpose is up to God. Fulfilling our purpose is up to us. And the first step to fulfilling it is finding it.

I believe that each of us has a general purpose and a specific purpose for our life. We need to understand both of them.

The Bible is very plain about the general purpose of every believer.

> Likewise, my brethren, you have undergone death as to the Law through the [crucified] body of Christ, so that now you may belong to Another, to Him Who was raised from the dead in order that we may bear fruit for God.
>
> Romans 7:4 AMP

Basically, this verse is saying that the general purpose of our life is to belong to Christ and to bear fruit for God. That's what it all boils down to.

How do we bear fruit?

We do that by using our God-given gifts and abilities to carry out the plan of God and be a blessing to others.

Each one should use whatever gift he has received
to serve others, faithfully administering God's grace
in its various forms.

1 Peter 4:10 NIV

Each of us has been given a form of God's grace so that
we can express His love and life to those around us. When
we discover what particular form that grace is to take in
our life, I believe that we've found our specific purpose.

Although many people agonize over discovering the
specific purpose of their life, it's not as difficult as we
may think. God has placed a major clue inside every
person. It's called our *gift* or *bent*.

Train up a child in the way he should go [and in
keeping with his individual gift or bent]....

Proverbs 22:6 AMP

Once we find out what our bent is, we're well on our
way to finding our purpose.

One dictionary defines "bent" as "...a strong inclination or interest...a special inclination or capacity:
talent."[5] It is a natural liking for an activity and the like-
lihood of succeeding in it.

It sounds pretty simple, but somehow many of us
manage to turn the discovery of our bent into something

complicated and confusing. We think that if we enjoy something or if it comes easily to us, it can't be God. We believe that the will of God for us has to be something we don't want to do, with people we don't want to do it with, in places we don't want to go. If it's something that appeals to us, it must not be God. We must have just thought it up ourselves.

That's not necessarily true. Certainly we have to guard against carnality and the desire to simply gratify our flesh, but giving us a particular bent was actually a very clever move on God's part. First of all, it provides us with a natural inspiration to obey Him. And secondly, it enables us to focus on flowing with Him rather than on having to concentrate on the mechanics of whatever we're doing.

It's similar to walking. Isn't it a blessing that we don't have to consciously think about the technical aspects of walking every time we want to walk somewhere? It's very natural to us—almost a reflex. We don't have to think about doing it, once we grow out of the early stages of development. We're free to focus our attention and energy on where we're going and what we're going to do when we get there.

God's not wasteful or haphazard. He's not going to take great care to specifically shape us and design us with certain abilities and aptitudes and then give us an assignment totally unrelated to that.

When we're walking with God, everything is strategic. He's not into busywork. Everywhere He leads us relates to His purpose for our life.

The life of David is a perfect example of what I'm talking about. God gave him a bent for shepherding.

> He chose David His servant and took him from the sheepfolds;
>
> From tending the ewes that had their young He brought him to be the shepherd of Jacob His people, of Israel His inheritance.
>
> So [David] was their shepherd with an upright heart; he guided them by the discernment and skillfulness [which controlled] his hands.
>
> Psalm 78:70-72 AMP

In his early years, David shepherded sheep. But that wasn't just something to keep him occupied until the "real" plan of God came along. That *was* the plan of God! God was grooming him all along for the day when he would shepherd people. Same bent, different flock.

Think about Peter. He grew up learning to catch fish. But all of that was simply for the purpose of grooming him to catch men (lead people to Jesus). Same bent, different pond.

Don't make this harder than it is. If you're having trouble finding your purpose in life, you can start by asking God to enlighten the "eyes of your understanding" about it. (See Eph. 1:18.) Then ask yourself a few simple questions: What am I good at? What do I like to do? What is my passion? Where do I seem to get the most results in my life? Just start there and then allow God to direct you to the next step.

THE NEXT STEP

We need to learn to take things one step at a time, because that's how God leads us.

> The steps of a good man are ordered by the Lord....
> Psalm 37:23 NIV

His leading is not in sporadic bursts or in quantum leaps, but in steps.

A step is simply a stage in a process. It's not an end in itself. It's just one piece of the puzzle.

That's why it's so important that we stay hooked up with God. He's the One who has the big picture! He knows the end from the beginning. (See Isa. 46:10.) He knows exactly how to position us so that we are in the right place at the right time with the right people to carry out every step in His course for us. Our steps are ordered in the appropriate sequence so that it will perfectly fulfill His plan.

God's not going to show us everything about His plan for our life all at once. (We probably couldn't handle it if He did!) But He will give us *something* that we can act on today. When He does, we need to do it—not when we get around to it, but *now*. And we need to do it wholeheartedly, regardless of how insignificant it may seem.

> Throw yourselves into the work of the Master, confident that nothing you do for Him is a waste of time or effort.
>
> 1 Corinthians 15:58 MESSAGE

Whatever season we're in, we need to make the most of it. That's how God prepares us for the next one. It's all interconnected. Each step leads to the next step. That's God's process for fulfilling His plan.

The great temptation is to try to speed up God's timetable or to try to skip steps. We want God to thrust us into the final phase of His plan for us almost before we've begun. We keep trying to work our way over to Step Z when we haven't even completed Step B yet.

How do we get caught up in this kind of thinking?

It's usually as a result of comparing ourselves with other people, something the Word of God specifically warns us against.

> ...when they measure themselves with themselves and compare themselves with one another, they are without understanding and behave unwisely.
>
> 2 Corinthians 10:12 AMP

Other people are never the standard or reference point for either our faith or our calling. We have to look to God for those things.

Jesus made that clear for us in the encounter He had with Peter.

> I assure you, most solemnly I tell you, when you were young you girded yourself [put on your own belt or girdle] and you walked about wherever you pleased to go. But when you grow old you will stretch out

your hands and someone else will put a girdle around you and carry you where you do not wish to go.

He said this to indicate by what kind of death Peter would glorify God. And after this He said to him, Follow Me!

But Peter turned and saw the disciple whom Jesus loved, following....

When Peter saw him, he said to Jesus, Lord, what about this man?

Jesus said to him, If I want him to stay (survive, live) till I come, what is that to you? [What concern is it of yours?] You follow Me!

John 21:18-22 AMP

Taking his eyes off of the Lord had gotten Peter in trouble before. (See Matt. 14:30,31.) He should have remembered the lesson.

When it comes to fulfilling the plan of God for our life, we have to keep our eyes on Jesus. It doesn't matter what anybody else thinks or says. It doesn't matter what their calling is or how God is using them. All that matters is that we personally follow Him—whatever He tells us to do, wherever He tells us to go, whenever He tells us to go there, every step of the way.

STAY ON COURSE

We've already looked at several passages that tell us how God has a predetermined course for our life. Paul reminds us of that again in his letter to the Ephesians.

> For we are God's [own] handiwork (His workmanship), recreated in Christ Jesus, [born anew] that we may do those good works which God predestined (planned beforehand) for us (taking paths which He prepared ahead of time) that we should walk in them [living the good life which He prearranged and made ready for us to live].
>
> Ephesians 2:10 AMP

God already has plans for us—great plans, awesome plans! They're ready and waiting. All we need to do is step into them.

But we don't have to. He won't make us. The choice is ours.

We need to understand something, though. If we *don't* follow His course for our life, if we insist on going our own way, we're in for a bumpy ride.

Why?

We'll be navigating in our own strength and wisdom—and that isn't very much to go on.

God is only going to fulfill *His* purpose for our life, not ours.

> The Lord will fulfill [his purpose] for me....
>
> Psalm 138:8 NIV

That's not because He's mean and stubborn. It's because He loves us too much to back a plan that's only going to hurt us in the long run. If we want to follow a plan like that, we'll have to carry it out on our own. He's not going to participate in it.

God's plan for us is the only one that will be able to stand up against the devil and the pressures of this life.

> Many plans are in a man's mind, but it is the Lord's purpose for him that will stand.
>
> Proverbs 19:21 AMP

It doesn't matter how smart we are. God's smarter. And if we give ourselves over to anything but *His* plan for our life, we're going to be disappointed and defeated, maybe even destroyed.

So let's just choose to go with God. Let's find our place, keep rank, and stay in step with Him. That's the path to victory.

PRINCIPLE #5

Love Mercy

The army was wracked by sectional rivalries...the troops 'would as soon fight each other as the enemy.'[1]
—GEORGE WASHINGTON,
cited by Burke Davis
George Washington and the American Revolution

One of [Anthony] Wayne's last warnings to Congress had been a forecast of disaster: '...I very much dread the Ides of January...it is not the prowess of the enemy I dread, but their taking advantage of our necessitous situation and internal disunion....'[2]
—BURKE DAVIS
George Washington and the American Revolution

...the day Grant told Smith to go back to New York, Rawlins sent a letter to Mrs. Rawlins: General Grant today relieved Major General William F. Smith from command and duty in this army, because of his spirit of criticism of all military movements and men, and his failure to get along with anyone he is placed under, and his disposition to scatter the seeds of discontent throughout the army.[3]
—BRUCE CATTON
Grant Takes Command

PRINCIPLE

LOVE MERCY

#5

Many believers spend all their lives worrying about whether or not they're pleasing God. They continually wring their hands over whether or not they're praying enough, fasting enough, reading their Bible enough, going to church enough, or giving enough. They assume that these "spiritual" things are a set of laws that God requires us to follow without fail, and they assume that more is better. They're just not sure how much more is necessary.

They could save themselves the frustration by simply turning to the book of Micah.

> With what shall I come before the Lord and bow down before the exalted God? Shall I come before him with burnt offerings, with calves a year old?
>
> Will the Lord be pleased with thousands of rams, with ten thousand rivers of oil? Shall I offer

my firstborn for my transgression, the fruit of my
body for the sin of my soul?

He has showed you, O man, what is good. And
what does the Lord require of you? To act justly and
to love mercy and to walk humbly with your God.

Micah 6:6-8 NIV

Pleasing God is not about following a bunch of rules
and regulations. It's about loving Him and loving people.

THE HEART OF GOD

It's not that there is anything wrong with praying
or fasting or reading the Bible or going to church or
giving or any number of other practices we could
mention. The Word of God encourages us to do all of
those things.

The danger is that we can do all of those things
without really caring about God or other people. Many
of the Pharisees were experts at it. It's called legalism,
and it doesn't represent the heart of God.

The heart of God is love. He loves people and takes
an active interest in helping them become everything
He created them to be.

Some of the Pharisees completely missed that point. They caught the letter of God's Law, but they missed the spirit of it.

They thought being righteous was all about who could follow the rules best. In fact, in an attempt to prove their spirituality and devotion to God, they even invented rules on top of the ones He had given them. Unfortunately, they allowed themselves to become so consumed with their rules that they forgot about people.

Jesus addressed this very issue with them twice in the book of Matthew.

> And as Jesus reclined at table in the house, behold, many tax collectors and [especially wicked] sinners came and sat (reclined) with Him and His disciples.
>
> And when the Pharisees saw this, they said to His disciples, Why does your Master eat with tax collectors and those [preeminently] sinful?
>
> But when Jesus heard it, He replied, Those who are strong and well (healthy) have no need of a physician, but those who are weak and sick.
>
> Go and learn what this means: I desire mercy [that is, readiness to help those in trouble] and not sacrifice and sacrificial victims. For I came not to call and invite [to repentance] the righteous (those

who are upright and in right standing with God), but sinners (the erring ones and all those not free from sin).

Matthew 9:10-13 AMP

At that particular time Jesus went through the fields of standing grain on the Sabbath; and His disciples were hungry, and they began to pick off the spikes of grain and to eat.

And when the Pharisees saw it, they said to Him, See there! Your disciples are doing what is unlawful and not permitted on the Sabbath.

He said to them, Have you not even read what David did when he was hungry, and those who accompanied him—

How he went into the house of God and ate the loaves of the showbread—which it was not lawful for him to eat, nor for the men who accompanied him, but for the priests only?

Or have you never read in the Law that on the Sabbath the priests in the temple violate the sanctity of the Sabbath [breaking it] and yet are guiltless?

But I tell you, Something greater and more exalted and more majestic than the temple is here!

And if you had only known what this saying means, I desire mercy [readiness to help, to spare, to forgive] rather than sacrifice and sacrificial victims, you would not have condemned the guiltless.

Matthew 12:1-7 AMP

Jesus wasn't really telling them anything new. This wasn't some wild doctrine He had just made up. He was simply reminding them of something God had already spoken to them back in the Old Testament.

For I desire mercy, not sacrifice, and acknowledgment of God rather than burnt offerings.

Hosea 6:6 NIV

They had heard all this before. They just weren't practicing it.

This issue actually became an ongoing source of conflict between Jesus and the Pharisees. They kept looking for opportunities to prove that their way was the correct way of pleasing God. And Jesus kept using those opportunities to prove that it wasn't.

Let's take a look at another familiar passage on this in the book of Matthew.

Now when the Pharisees heard that He had silenced (muzzled) the Sadducees, they gathered together.

And one of their number, a lawyer, asked Him a question to test Him.

Teacher, which kind of commandment is great and important (the principal kind) in the Law?...

And He replied to him, You shall love the Lord your God with all your heart and with all your soul and with all your mind (intellect).

This is the great (most important, principal) and first commandment.

And a second is like it: You shall love your neighbor as [you do] yourself.

These two commandments sum up and upon them depends all the Law and the prophets.

Matthew 22:34-40 AMP

Again, Jesus wasn't telling them anything new. This wasn't something they hadn't heard before. He was simply quoting two passages from the Law—Deuteronomy 6:5 and Leviticus 19:18—passages they all knew quite well.

Jesus said that the essence of God's Law is to love God and to love people. Everything else flows from those principles.

The Pharisees knew that in their heads. It just hadn't filtered down to their hearts.

THE SPIRIT OF JONAH

The problem was that some of the Pharisees had what we might call the spirit of Jonah. They loved judgment more than mercy. To understand this concept a little better we're going to look at the story of Jonah.

I'm sure you recall how Jonah had run away from God's call on him to preach repentance to Ninevah. It took a three-day stay in the belly of a great fish before Jonah finally headed to Ninevah and obeyed God.

On the first day, Jonah started into the city. He proclaimed: "Forty more days and Ninevah will be overturned."

The Ninevites believed God. They declared a fast, and all of them, from the greatest to the least, put on sackcloth.

When the news reached the king of Ninevah, he rose from his throne, took off his royal robes, covered himself with sackcloth and sat down in the dust.

Then he issued a proclamation in Ninevah....

"...let man and beast be covered with sackcloth. Let everyone call urgently on God. Let them give up their evil ways and their violence.

Who knows? God may yet relent and with compassion turn from His fierce anger so that we will not perish."

When God saw what they did and how they turned from their evil ways, he had compassion and did not bring upon them the destruction he had threatened.

Jonah 3:4-10 NIV

Seeing a whole city turn to God should have thrilled Jonah, but his heart was filled with judgment instead of mercy.

But Jonah was greatly displeased and became angry.

He prayed to the Lord, "O Lord, is this not what I said when I was still at home? That is why I was so quick to flee to Tarshish. I knew that you are a gracious and compassionate God, slow to anger and abounding in love, a God who relents from sending calamity.

Now, O Lord, take away my life, for it is better for me to die than to live."

But the Lord replied, "Have you any right to be angry?"

Jonah went out and sat down at a place east of the city. There he made himself a shelter, sat in its shade and waited to see what would happen to the city.

Then the Lord God provided a vine and made it grow up over Jonah to give shade for his head to ease his discomfort, and Jonah was very happy about the vine.

But at dawn the next day God provided a worm, which chewed the vine so that it withered.

When the sun rose, God provided a scorching east wind, and the sun blazed on Jonah's head so that he grew faint. He wanted to die, and said, "It would be better for me to die than to live."

But God said to Jonah, "Do you have a right to be angry about the vine?" "I do," he said. "I am angry enough to die."

But the Lord said, "You have been concerned about this vine, though you did not tend it or make it grow. It sprang up overnight and died overnight.

But Ninevah has more than a hundred and twenty thousand people who cannot tell their right hand from their left, and many cattle as well. Should I not be concerned about that great city?"

Jonah 4:1-11 NIV

Obviously, Jonah's perspective and God's perspective were miles apart. Jonah had clearly lost sight of the heart of God.

The first chapter of the book of Jonah tells how Jonah rebelled against the call of God to go to Ninevah. As we saw earlier, that rebellion landed him in the belly of a whale. After a few days of soul-searching in that environment,

Jonah decided to make the trip after all. But we can tell by his words that his heart really hadn't changed.

People often refer to this incident as a matter of Jonah resisting the call of God to preach. It seems to me that it wasn't so much that he didn't want to preach; he just didn't want to preach to *those* people.

The fact is that Ninevah was the capital city of Assyria, and Assyria was one of Israel's most detested enemies. Jonah didn't want God to have mercy on them. He wanted God to "get 'em."[4]

Ever been there? Ever had somebody offend you one too many times? Ever felt like blasting off on somebody—at least verbally, if not physically? Ever taken pleasure in the thought that someday that person was going to "get theirs"?

We can probably all relate to those feelings. And we can probably all find plenty of reasons to justify ourselves for having them. We just need to understand that God doesn't see it that way.

It is clear in the Bible that God loves people and takes no pleasure in judging them.

> Who is a God like You, Who forgives iniquity and passes over the transgression of the remnant of His

heritage? He retains not His anger forever, because He delights in mercy and loving-kindness.

Micah 7:18 AMP

Have I any pleasure in the death of the wicked? says the Lord, and not rather that he should turn from his evil way and return [to his God] and live?

Ezekiel 18:23 AMP

God has a significant investment in each one of us. We were uniquely created by Him, and we have a special assignment from Him. He considers us far too valuable to simply toss away without a second thought—even when it appears that there doesn't seem to be much there worth salvaging.

Jonah couldn't relate to that. For one thing, he didn't have a personal investment in the people of Ninevah; to him, they were expendable. He grieved more over not having a little shade from the sun than he grieved over the fate of the more than 120,000 souls in that city.

How did that happen? How did a prophet of God get so far off the mark?

One of the main reasons is, he forgot His purpose. He forgot that he was there to love God and to love people.

If we forget our purpose, we'll fall into the same error today.

Notice that Micah 7:18 says that God "*delights* in mercy." He doesn't just dispense it once in awhile for a little change of pace between acts of judgment. He delights in it. That's His nature. That's the way He is— not just sometimes; all the time.

If we need more evidence of that, all we have to do is turn to the book of Psalms. In Psalm 136 alone, each of the twenty-six verses ends with the phrase "...for His mercy endureth forever." And there are many more passages throughout this wonderful book that refer to the mercy of God.

Two of the best known are found in Psalm 103 and Psalm 145.

> The Lord is merciful and gracious, slow to anger
> and plenteous in mercy and loving-kindness.
>
> Psalm 103:8 AMP

> The Lord is gracious and full of compassion, slow
> to anger and abounding in mercy and loving-kindness.
>
> Psalm 145:8 AMP

Merciful, gracious, slow to anger, full of compassion, plenteous in and abounding in mercy and loving-kindness—that's the nature of God.

The interesting thing is that Jonah knew about God's nature. In fact, he specifically mentioned the attributes referred to in these passages in his conversation with God. (See Jonah 4:2.) He just wanted God to make an exception in this case.

Many of us have a tendency to be a lot harder on other people than we are on ourselves. We often forget about all the mistakes *we've* made. We forget about all the times that *we've* missed it. We forget about all the times that *we've* had to ask God for forgiveness about something. But to us that's okay because we know that God understands that *we* really didn't mean it, that *we* didn't realize what we were doing at the time. It was just a little slip, a moment of weakness.

But those *other* people...*they're* different. *They* need to be taught a lesson. *They* deserve to be punished.

The reality is that they probably do deserve to be punished, but they've been given grace and mercy.

When?

The same time we were—when Jesus was crucified on the cross. He took the punishment for *everyone's* sin so that everyone could receive the benefit of God's mercy.

We didn't earn it. We didn't deserve it. The Word says that God just did it because He loved us.

> But God—so rich is He in His mercy! Because of and in order to satisfy the great and wonderful and intense love with which He loved us,
>
> Even when we were dead (slain) by [our own] shortcomings and trespasses, He made us alive together in fellowship and in union with Christ; [He gave us the very life of Christ Himself, the same new life with which He quickened Him, for] it is by grace (His favor and mercy which you did not deserve) that you are saved (delivered from judgment and made partakers of Christ's salvation).
>
> Ephesians 2:4,5 AMP

God didn't just take a skin-deep look at us and then throw up His hands in disgust. He wasn't put off by our sin and degradation. He looked beyond all that and saw us the way we *could* be in Him.

If we're going to stay in step with God as believers, we're going to have to start seeing people in that same way—with eyes of love that see past what they are to what they could be in Him.

SEEING FROM GOD'S PERSPECTIVE

Jesus brought this truth home in a powerful way one evening when He was having dinner in the home of a Pharisee named Simon.

While they were eating, a woman—one whom the Scripture says had lived a very sinful life—came in to wipe Jesus' feet and anoint them with perfume. Simon was appalled, but Jesus used the opportunity to teach him something about the heart of God.

> When the Pharisee who had invited him saw this, he said to himself, "If this man were a prophet, he would know who is touching him and what kind of woman she is—that she is a sinner."
>
> Jesus answered him, "Simon, I have something to tell you." "Tell me, teacher," he said.
>
> "Two men owed money to a certain money-lender. One owed him five hundred denarii, and the other fifty.

Neither of them had the money to pay him back, so he canceled the debts of both. Now which of them will love him more?"

Simon replied, "I suppose the one who had the bigger debt canceled." "You have judged correctly," Jesus said.

Then he turned toward the woman and said to Simon, "Do you see this woman? I came into your house. You did not give me any water for my feet, but she wet my feet with her tears and wiped them with her hair.

You did not give me a kiss, but this woman, from the time I entered, has not stopped kissing my feet.

You did not put oil on my head, but she has poured perfume on my feet.

Therefore, I tell you, her many sins have been forgiven—for she loved much. But he who has been forgiven little loves little."

Luke 7:39-47 NIV

If we stop and look at the story a little more closely, we'll see that it wasn't just a lesson for Simon. It's a lesson for all of us.

In sharing the parable about the two men who owed money, Jesus painted an interesting picture. One man owed a lot. One man owed a little. But the point is that *neither* of them could pay their debt. They *both* needed mercy.

Sometimes it's easy to slip into the mind-set that our sins and failures aren't really all *that* bad—at least, not as bad as Brother so-and-so's. But the bottom line for us is the same as it was for the men in the parable: We all owe a debt to God we can't pay. We are all in need of His mercy; no exceptions.

The amount of the debt is irrelevant. Think of it this way. Let's say the price of admission to a particular event is $10. If that's the case, it doesn't matter if you walk up to the ticket window with $9 or with $1. Unless you have $10, you're not going to get a ticket, and they're not going to let you in the door.

The same concept applies in attempting to justify ourselves according to some kind of sinfulness scale—it is a waste of time. God is not impressed by how sinless we think we are compared to other people. He is the *only* Standard, and the Bible says that we have *all* fallen short of it.

> For all have sinned; all fall short of God's glorious standard.

Yet now God in his gracious kindness declares us not guilty. He has done this through Christ Jesus, who has freed us by taking away our sins.

For God sent Jesus to take the punishment for our sins and to satisfy God's anger against us. We are made right with God when we believe that Jesus shed his blood, sacrificing his life for us....

Romans 3:23-25 NLT

The *only* reason we can stand justified before God is because of the blood of Jesus.

It really doesn't matter what we've done or haven't done. It really doesn't matter what particular sins we've committed. The truth is that we're all in the same desperate spiritual condition apart from God: lost and without hope.

No one is better than anyone else. We're all in need of a Savior. We're all nothing apart from Him. If we ever forget that, we'll end up squandering our days making petty comparisons with people instead of loving them.

Remember the question Jesus asked Simon in Luke 7:44 NIV: "Do you see this woman?"

On the surface it almost sounds silly. Of course he could see her! She was standing right there.

But Jesus wasn't talking about natural vision. He was talking about spiritual vision. He was talking about seeing things from God's perspective—and He knew Simon didn't.

Jesus knew that Simon didn't really see this woman. All Simon saw was her sin.

Jesus knew that Simon didn't really see her pain or her suffering or her desperation. All Simon saw was the result of it. And because of that, Simon's heart was too hardened to make way for the love of God to be released.

When Jesus said that those who have been forgiven little love little, He was speaking from man's perspective of degrees of sin. The truth is that we have all been forgiven much.

Perception is everything. If we perceive—as Simon did—that we've only been forgiven little, that we weren't really that bad before God came along anyway, that we can handle our lives without His help (most of the time anyway, except in emergencies), then we're going to love little. God's not going to matter that much to us and neither will people.

But if we perceive—correctly—that I have been forgiven much, that apart from Him we are nothing and can do nothing, that we owe everything to Him, then it's a totally different picture in which God does matter to us. And when God matters to us, people matter to us because they matter to Him.

If we want to please God and be useful to Him, then we have to realize that love and mercy are no longer optional for us; they're mandatory.

> If I speak in the tongues of men and of angels, but have not love, I am only a resounding gong or a clanging cymbal.
>
> If I have the gift of prophecy and can fathom all mysteries and all knowledge, and if I have a faith that can move mountains, but have not love, I am nothing.
>
> If I give all I possess to the poor and surrender my body to the flames, but have not love, I gain nothing.
>
> 1 Corinthians 13:1-3 NIV

> For [if we are] in Christ Jesus, neither circumcision nor uncircumcision counts for anything, but only faith activated and energized and expressed and working through love.
>
> Galatians 5:6 AMP

> Dear friends, let us love one another, for love comes from God. Everyone who loves has been born of God and knows God.

Whoever does not love does not know God, because God is love.

This is how God showed his love among us: He sent his one and only Son into the world that we might live through him.

This is love: not that we loved God, but that he loved us and sent his Son as an atoning sacrifice for our sins.

Dear friends, since God so loved us, we also ought to love one another.

1 John 4:7-11 NIV

God is love, and He intends for love to be the centerpiece of all our relationships and of all that we say and do.

But love isn't just the goal of our service. It's the only effective and enduring motivation for it.

Jesus answered, If a person [really] loves Me, he will keep My word [obey My teaching]....

John 14:23 AMP

Greater love hath no man than this, that a man lay down his life for his friends.

John 15:13

We loved you so much that we were delighted to share with you not only the gospel of God but our lives as well, because you had become so dear to us.

1 Thessalonians 2:8 NIV

Nothing motivates like love. Rules won't do it. Guilt won't do it. Emotion won't do it. Only love has the power to compel us to great service. And the greater the love, the greater the service.

STRIFE DESTROYS;
LOVE UNITES

Real love is powerful. It's dynamic! In fact, according to the Word of God, love is virtually an unstoppable force.

...for love is strong as death....

Many waters cannot quench love, neither can the floods drown it....

Song of Solomon 8:6,7

No doubt that's why the devil does everything he possibly can to keep the Church enmeshed in strife.

Throughout history, one of the fundamental principles of war strategy has been "divide and conquer," because there is obvious strength in unity.

Two are better than one, because they have a
good return for their work:

If one falls down, his friend can help him up.
But pity the man who falls and has no one to help
him up!

Though one may be overpowered, two can
defend themselves. A cord of three strands is not
quickly broken.

Ecclesiastes 4:9,10,12 NIV

That's not just true in the natural realm. That's true
in the spiritual realm as well.

But there's something unique about the unity of
believers. This kind of spiritual unity is so powerful that
the Bible actually compares it to the anointing of God.

How good and pleasant it is when brothers live
together in unity!

It is like precious oil poured on the head, running
down on the beard, running down on Aaron's beard,
down upon the collar of his robes.

Psalm 133:1,2 NIV

The oil spoken of in these verses refers to the
anointing oil used to consecrate the priest to the service
of God and release the power of God upon his life to
minister in that office.[5]

With that in mind, we could say that when we walk in unity, we release the power of God to flow through us into whatever situation we may be facing.

In other words, unity is a spiritual catalyst. It helps create an environment in which the power of God can operate freely and unhindered.

Jesus makes this point a little more clearly in Matthew 18:19-20.

> Again I say unto you, That if two of you shall agree on earth as touching any thing that they shall ask, it shall be done for them of my Father which is in heaven.
>
> For where two or three are gathered together in my name, there am I in the midst of them.

For believers, unity is not about simply gathering together in a crowd. It's about believing, praying, and agreeing together in faith and bringing the power of God on the scene. And when God comes on the scene, things happen! Lives change. Families are restored. Sicknesses are healed. Destinies are fulfilled. It's wonderful!

But it's a nightmare for the kingdom of darkness. And because the devil takes that kind of thing very seriously, we can expect him to go to great lengths to keep believers out of harmony with each other.

One of his favorite ploys is what the Bible refers to as "fiery darts."

> Above all, taking the shield of faith, wherewith ye shall be able to quench all the fiery darts of the wicked.
>
> Ephesians 6:16

Although fiery darts aren't limited to the arena of strife, we can expect a full-scale onslaught of them there due to the strategic importance of the issue.

What do we mean by fiery darts?

The word fiery means "...liable to catch fire or explode...."[6] So, in this case, we could say that fiery darts are those irritating and annoying incidents in our lives that the devil would like to light a match to in hopes of creating some kind of interpersonal explosion.

We've all been there. Somebody says something they shouldn't have said. Somebody does something they shouldn't have done. Next thing you know, we're ticked off! We're upset! We're definitely in a situation which is "liable to [likely to] catch fire or explode."

What the devil doesn't want us to know is that we are the ones who determine whether or not that explosion occurs—not God, not the other person, not even the devil.

It's been said that we each carry two buckets to the scene of every conflict. One bucket contains gasoline. The other contains water.

If we respond with emotional gasoline, we will ignite an explosion of strife and anger that may become difficult—if not impossible—to control and will likely result in serious damage to everyone concerned.

If, on the other hand, we respond with the purifying water of the Word (see Eph. 5:26), we will release a flow of the power of God that can bring healing and forgiveness and restoration into the situation.

Let's be honest. At times our flesh may relish the thought of indulging in a few juicy moments of strife with someone, especially when we've been wronged or misunderstood.

But if we want to walk in victory, we must determine once and for all that strife is not our friend—not now, not ever.

> For where envying and strife is, there is confusion and every evil work.
>
> James 3:16

> And if a kingdom be divided against itself, that kingdom cannot stand.

And if a house be divided against itself, that house cannot stand.

Mark 3:24,25

Notice the wording again in the passage in Mark 3. It doesn't say *might* not stand, but "*cannot* stand." In other words, strife brings inevitable destruction.

Unlike love, there are no benefits in strife. It's not simply a harmless emotional release. It's deadly. It will drag us down to certain defeat. It's a luxury no first-class soldier can afford.

PRINCIPLE #6

WALK HUMBLY

If one were to select a single factor that lost the Confederates this battle [of Gettysburg] the choice would probably be Stuart's absence at a critical time.... If it is agreed that Stuart's escapade lost Lee the battle through causing him to fight it partially blind, it illustrates once again how disastrous can be lack of accurate information, and it shows how a personal characteristic—vanity—can influence the course of a battle.[1]

—WILLIAM SEYMOUR
Decisive Factors in Twenty
Great Battles of the World

Alexander the Great was a master of innovation, he constantly surprised his enemies by the novel application of tactics and techniques. He developed a technique of surprising his enemies on the battlefield by attacking them at their strongest point.[2]

—COLONEL MICHAEL DEWAR
The Art of Deception in Warfare

PRINCIPLE

WALK HUMBLY

#6

God is a winner, and He wants His people to be winners—not just when we get to heaven, but now, today, in this life. That's not just one of those feel-good doctrines somebody made up in order to create a following for themselves. It's plainly stated in the Bible.

> The Lord will open the heavens, the store-house of his bounty, to send rain on your land in season and to bless all the work of your hands. You will lend to many nations but will borrow from none.

> The Lord will make you the head, not the tail. If you pay attention to the commands of the Lord your God that I give you this day and carefully follow them, you will always be at the top, never at the bottom.

> Deuteronomy 28:12,13 NIV

> In the Messiah, in Christ, God leads us from place
> to place in one perpetual victory parade....
>
> 2 Corinthians 2:14 MESSAGE

We could cite many more passages on this subject, but these are sufficient to reveal God's heart on the matter.

The danger is that as we begin to progress from victory to victory, we tend to forget how we got there. And once we forget that, it's the beginning of the end of our "winning streak."

"TILL HE WAS STRONG"

King Uzziah is a classic example of someone whose victory parade came to a screeching halt. We find his story in 2 Chronicles 26.

> Uzziah was sixteen years old when he began his fifty-two year reign in Jerusalem....
>
> He did right in the Lord's sight, to the extent of all that his father Amaziah did.
>
> He set himself to seek God in the days of Zechariah, who instructed him in the things of God; and as long as he sought (inquired of, yearned for) the Lord, God made him prosper.
>
> He went out against the Philistines and broke down the walls of Gath, of Jabneh, and of Ashdod,

and built cities near Ashdod and elsewhere among the Philistines.

The Ammonites paid tribute to Uzziah, and his fame spread abroad even to the border of Egypt, for he became very strong.

Also Uzziah built towers in Jerusalem at the Corner Gate, the Valley Gate, and at the angle of the wall, and fortified them.

Also he built towers in the wilderness and hewed out many cisterns, for he had much livestock....

And Uzziah had a combat army for waging war....

...And his fame spread far, for he was marvelously helped till he was strong.

But when [King Uzziah] was strong, he became proud to his destruction; and he trespassed against the Lord his God, for he went into the temple of the Lord to burn incense on the altar of incense.

And Azariah the priest went in after him and with him eighty priests of the Lord, men of courage.

They opposed King Uzziah and said to him, It is not for you, Uzziah, to burn incense to the Lord, but for the priests, the sons of Aaron, who are set apart to burn incense. Withdraw from the sanctuary; you have trespassed, and that will not be to your credit and honor before the Lord God.

Then Uzziah was enraged, and he had a censer in his hand to burn incense. And while he was enraged with the priests, leprosy broke out on his forehead before the priests in the house of the Lord, beside the incense altar.

And as Azariah the chief priest and all the priests looked upon him, behold, he was leprous on his forehead! So they forced him out of there; and he also made haste to get out, because the Lord had smitten him.

And King Uzziah was a leper to the day of his death, and, being a leper, he dwelt in a separate house, for he was excluded from the Lord's house. And Jotham his son took charge of the king's household, ruling the people of the land.

2 Chronicles 26:3-6,8-11,15-21 AMP

Imagine, fifty-two years of success after success, victory followed by victory, blessing heaped upon blessing—and Uzziah lost it all in a moment because he forgot how it happened!

We must always remember that God is the Source of our victory—not our own wisdom, not our own cleverness, not our own strength, not our own talent, not our own ability—God and God alone.

We have heard with our ears, O God; our fathers have told us what you did in their days, in days long ago.

With your hand you drove out the nations and planted our fathers; you crushed the peoples and made our fathers flourish.

It was not by their sword that they won the land, nor did their arm bring them victory; it was your right hand, your arm, and the light of your face, for you loved them.

You are my King and my God, who decrees victories for Jacob.

Through you we push back our enemies; through your name we trample our foes.

I do not trust in my bow, my sword does not bring me victory;

but you give us victory over our enemies, you put our adversaries to shame.

In God we make our boast all day long, and we will praise your name forever. Selah

Psalm 44:1-8 NIV

The horse is made ready for the day of battle, but victory rests with the Lord.

Proverbs 21:31 NIV

God's the One with the wisdom. He's the One with the plan. He's the One with the power. The only thing we supply is the obedience.

And we couldn't even do that without God. The apostle Paul tells us that even our ability and desire to obey come from the Lord:

> [Not in your own strength] for it is God Who is all the while effectually at work in you [energizing and creating in you the power and desire], both to will and to work for His good pleasure and satisfaction and delight.
>
> Philippians 2:13 AMP

Because this is such a crucial issue, Paul touches on it to some degree in most of his writings. But perhaps nowhere does he state his case more plainly than in his first letter to the Corinthian church.

> What makes you better than anyone else? What do you have that God hasn't given you? And if all you have is from God, why boast as though you have accomplished something on your own?
>
> 1 Corinthians 4:7 NLT

Sometimes we treat God as though He were the spiritual equivalent of training wheels. Remember training wheels? They're those special small, supplementary wheels that can be attached to the rear axle of a bicycle to help provide a little extra stability and safety while the rider learns the basics of pedaling, steering, and maintaining balance. Eventually the rider becomes so accomplished that the training wheels can be discarded. They've served their purpose. They're no longer needed. The rider can get along fine without them. In fact, that's the whole idea—to eventually get rid of them.

That's the way King Uzziah ended up seeing God— he thought that he didn't need God's help anymore. Oh, he knew it was important to stay close to God in the beginning. After all, Uzziah was just getting started then. He was only sixteen. He obviously still had a lot to learn.

The problem was that eventually the day came when Uzziah believed he was through learning. He looked around and saw that he had accomplished quite a bit over the years. He had gained quite a reputation for himself. In a word, he felt he had arrived. He didn't think he needed anyone's help anymore, not even God's. He figured he could get along fine on his own.

What a gross miscalculation! The king couldn't have been more wrong, as the rest of the story dramatically and tragically illustrates.

What Uzziah really needed was a good old-fashioned reality check, perhaps something like the one God provided for Job.

Job was a righteous man who lost his family, his wealth, and his health all in one day. Then while he sat "among the ashes," he was visited by three of his friends who came to mourn with him and to offer their ideas on why he had experienced such misfortune. His three friends implied that his suffering was the result of sin, but Job insisted on his innocence. Then God spoke to Job.

Then the Lord answered Job out of the storm. He said:

"Who is this that darkens my counsel with words without knowledge?

"Where were you when I laid the earth's foundation? Tell me, if you understand.

Who marked off its dimensions? Surely you know!

Have you comprehended the vast expanses of the earth? Tell me, if you know all this.

"What is the way to the abode of light? And where does darkness reside?

Can you take them to their places? Do you know the paths to their dwellings?

Surely you know, for you were already born! You have lived so many years!

Can you bring forth the constellations in their seasons...?

Do you know the laws of the heavens?...

Do you send the lightning bolts on their way? Do they report to you, 'Here we are'?"

Job 38:1,2,4,5,18-21,32-33,35 NIV

Job got the point. When God eventually gave him an opportunity to speak, Job humbly responded.

"...how can I reply to you? I put my hand over my mouth.

...Surely I spoke of things I did not understand, things too wonderful for me to know.

My ears had heard of you but now my eyes have seen you.

Therefore I despise myself and repent in dust and ashes."

Job 40:4; 42:3,5,6 NIV

Keep in mind that in this life-changing encounter, God's intention wasn't to embarrass or humiliate Job. He wanted to upgrade Job's perspective.

Basically, God's message to Job was, "I'm God and you're not." That was good advice for Job, and it's good advice for us.

THE SIN OF SODOM

If someone asked us to identify the sin committed by the people of Sodom, some might say that it was homosexuality, based on the account of Sodom's destruction described in Genesis 19. Verses 4-5 seem to support that conclusion.

A look at another Scripture, one of the passages in Ezekiel 16, sheds a little more light on the story.

> Behold, this was the iniquity of your sister Sodom: pride, overabundance of food, prosperous ease, and idleness were hers and her daughters'; neither did she strengthen the hand of the poor and needy.
>
> And they were haughty and committed abominable offenses before Me; therefore I removed them when I saw it and I saw fit.
>
> Ezekiel 16:49,50 AMP

This passage suggests that the real problem in Sodom was that life was all about them and pleasing themselves. Homosexuality was just one of the by-products. The root sin was pride.

One of the most dangerous things about pride is that it causes us to lose perspective and to think more highly of ourselves than we ought to think. Once that happens, we're headed for a fall.

That fact is stated repeatedly in the Word of God.

When pride comes, then comes disgrace, but
with humility comes wisdom.

Proverbs 11:2 NIV

Pride goes before destruction, a haughty spirit
before a fall.

Proverbs 16:18 NIV

A man's pride brings him low, but a man of lowly
spirit gains honor.

Proverbs 29:23 NIV

These verses on pride are straightforward enough.
Yet in spite of such clear warnings, many people seem
ever-susceptible to the temptation of exalting themselves over God and others.

You may be thinking, *Others maybe, but surely not God.*

The fact is, the whole issue of obedience is thoroughly intertwined with the issue of pride. They're
inseparable because obedience isn't simply about following instructions. It's about submitting to authority.

The dictionary bears this out. The word *obedient* is
defined as "submissive to the restraint or command of
authority..." or "...submissive to the will of another...."[3]

The one question we face every time we encounter temptation of any kind is, *Who is in charge of my life? Is God or am I? Will I submit my will to His or will I choose to do things my way?* That's really what it all comes down to.

Let's go to the story of King Saul for a closer look at God's perspective on this.

> Samuel said, When you were small in your own sight, were you not made the head of the tribes of Israel, and the Lord anointed you king over Israel?
>
> And the Lord sent you on a mission....
>
> Why then did you not obey the voice of the Lord...?
>
> Samuel said, Has the Lord as great a delight in burnt offerings and sacrifices as in obeying the voice of the Lord? Behold, to obey is better than sacrifice, and to hearken than the fat of rams.
>
> For rebellion is as the sin of witchcraft, and stubbornness is as idolatry.... Because you have rejected the word of the Lord, He also has rejected you from being king.
>
> 1 Samuel 15:17-19,22-23 AMP

Those are powerful words that present a powerful lesson. Too bad Saul never learned it.

Although Saul was king of Israel, that only made him God's servant, not His peer. God already had a plan for this situation and had clearly expressed His will to Saul about it. God didn't need Saul's input; He needed Saul's obedience.

Instead, Saul thought he had a better idea. He made a few adjustments—minor ones, in his opinion—and came up with a whole new plan.

God was unimpressed. In fact, Saul's "better" idea cost him the kingdom.

We need to understand something about the nature of sin. Whenever we sin (even in what we might consider to be minor ways), we're actually rebelling against God, despite the fact that we're probably not consciously intending it. We're refusing His will and insisting on our own will instead, which is like saying that we're right, and He's wrong; we're in charge, and He's not.

In verse 23 God likens this kind of behavior to idolatry—and we are the idol.

Being in pride is like playing God. We're making up the rules; we're deciding what's right and what's wrong. It doesn't matter what anyone else thinks. We're the boss. The only thing that matters is what we want.

That's what happened to the people of Sodom, and that's what happened to Saul. They decided to be in charge. They decided to make up the rules. They just didn't realize that when they did, they put themselves in a no-win situation.

Pride always leads to presumption, and that's a very dangerous place to be.

> Keep back Your servant also from presumptuous sins; let them not have dominion over me! Then shall I be blameless, and I shall be innocent and clear of great transgression.
>
> Psalm 19:13 AMP

It may not be clear whether the writer here means to say that "presumptuous sins" *are* great transgressions or that they simply *lead* to great transgressions, but it really doesn't matter. Either way we look at it, the connotation is obviously negative.

What do we mean by "presumptuous sins"?

Let's start with some definitions. The dictionary tells us that "presumptuous" means "overstepping due bounds as of propriety or courtesy: taking liberties."[4] It comes from the root word *presume,* which means "...to dare...assume...to undertake without leave or justification...to suppose to be true without proof...to take for granted...to go beyond what is right or proper."[5]

Barnes' Notes commentary says, "...The word [presumptuous] does not mean open sins, or flagrant sins, so much as those which spring from self-reliance or pride...."[6]

With these definitions in mind, we can say that King Uzziah and King Saul were both guilty of presumptuous sin. They misjudged their positions and claimed privileges to which they weren't entitled. They developed an exaggerated opinion of themselves and took their place in God for granted. They assumed they could bend (or break) the rules, and God would look the other way because they were important people.

But they were mistaken.

God doesn't owe us anything. Everything we enjoy in Him is due solely to His love for us and His grace, not our own merit. Therefore, the appropriate response on our part is gratitude and humility, not arrogance and presumption.

Second Chronicles gives us an account of King Hezekiah that touches on this very issue.

> In those days Hezekiah became ill and was at the point of death. He prayed to the Lord, who answered him and gave him a miraculous sign.

But Hezekiah's heart was proud and he did not respond to the kindness shown him; therefore the Lord's wrath was on him and on Judah and Jerusalem.

Then Hezekiah repented of the pride in his heart, as did the people of Jerusalem; therefore the Lord's wrath did not come upon them during the days of Hezekiah.

2 Chronicles 32:24-26 NIV

God was looking for a response to the immense kindness He had shown Hezekiah. Haughtiness wasn't exactly what He had in mind.

The good news is that Hezekiah repented of his prideful attitude and was restored to fellowship with God.

Unfortunately, the Scriptures do not give us any indication of the same for Saul or Uzziah. As far as we know, they never repented. As a result, they both failed to fulfill their God-given destinies, and their lives came to tragic, disappointing ends.

SUBMIT TO GOD

Although we've seen that pride is not an unpardonable sin, it's certainly nothing to play around with. For one thing, the Bible tells us that it puts us in direct conflict with God.

...."God resists the proud, but gives grace to the humble."

Therefore submit to God. Resist the devil and he will flee from you.

James 4:6,7 NKJV

Why would we want to alienate ourselves from the very One whose help we need the most? If there is anyone we want on our side, it's God!

We're far better off submitting ourselves to God and saving our resistance for the devil. Actually that's part of God's formula for success. Not only is it spiritually correct; it's just smart.

Paul basically tells us that in his letter to the church at Rome.

I appeal to you therefore, brethren, and beg of you in view of [all] the mercies of God, to make a decisive dedication of your bodies [presenting all your members and faculties] as a living sacrifice, holy (devoted, consecrated) and well pleasing to God, which is your reasonable (rational, intelligent) service and spiritual worship.

Romans 12:1 AMP

In other words, submitting ourselves completely to God and His will is the only fitting, reasonable, and appropriate response to who He is and all He has done for us. Anything else just doesn't make sense.

The way to go from victory to victory in life is to stop competing with God for the role of Commander in Chief. There's room for only one Lord—and He's it.

The Message Bible summarizes the matter in Romans 11:34-36:

> Is there anyone around who can explain God? Anyone smart enough to tell him what to do?
>
> Anyone who has done him such a huge favor that God has to ask his advice?"
>
> Everything comes from him;
>
> Everything happens through him;
>
> Everything ends up in him.
>
> Always glory! Always praise!
>
> Yes. Yes. Yes.

CONCLUSION
REFLECTIONS ON
SEPTEMBER 11, 2001

At the beginning of this book, we saw that what's happening in the world is not really about politics or economics. It's about darkness versus light; evil versus good.

The message that's been presented in these pages has dealt primarily with how to walk in victory on a personal level. But it's important for us to understand that the same God who is more than enough to cause us to triumph over evil in our personal lives is more than enough to triumph over evil on the world scene.

We don't have to worry about it; we don't have to wonder. The Bible makes it very clear that righteousness will be victorious in the end. Here's one of many passages that refers to our victory.

> Fret not yourself because of evildoers, neither be envious against those who work unrighteousness (that which is not upright or in right standing with God).

141

For they shall soon be cut down like the grass, and wither as the green herb.

Trust (lean on, rely on, and be confident) in the Lord and do good; so shall you dwell in the land and feed surely on His faithfulness, and truly you shall be fed.

And He will make your uprightness and right standing with God go forth as the light, and your justice and right as [the shining sun of] the noonday.

For evildoers shall be cut off, but those who wait and hope and look for the Lord [in the end] shall inherit the earth.

Psalm 37:1-3,7,9 AMP

No matter how bad it looks in the natural, God will never allow a fallen angel (Satan, who was foolish enough to get himself kicked out of heaven) to win in the end.[1] It's just not going to happen.

THE ONE TRUE GOD

The above passage tells us to feed on the faithfulness of God. That's good advice, and there's great encouragement in that. It will build our faith and help to keep us out of fear.

Not long before he died, Joshua reminded the children of Israel about the faithfulness of God.

> And behold, this day I am going the way of all the earth. Know in all your hearts and in all your souls that not one thing has failed of all the good things which the Lord your God promised concerning you. All have come to pass for you; not one thing of them has failed.
>
> Joshua 23:14

What good news! The same God who kept His Word then is keeping His Word now. And not one thing that He has promised will fail to come to pass.

We can see testimonies of it already happening all around us.

For example, one of the greatest testimonies to His faithfulness is the return of the Jews to Israel in this past century. In fact, God Himself seems to suggest in Isaiah 43:9-13 that this particular sign is actually evidence that He is God.

> All the nations gather together and the peoples assemble. Which of them foretold this and proclaimed to us the former things? Let them bring in their witnesses to prove they were right, so that others may hear and say, "It is true."

"You are my witnesses," declares the LORD, "and my servant whom I have chosen, so that you may know and believe me and understand that I am he. Before me no god was formed, nor will there be one after me.

I, even I, am the LORD, and apart from me there is no savior.

I have revealed and saved and proclaimed-I, and not some foreign god among you. You are my witnesses," declares the LORD, "that I am God.

Yes, and from ancient days I am he. No one can deliver out of my hand. When I act, who can reverse it?"

Isaiah 43:9-13 NIV

As we will see in the verses below, God foretold the re-gathering of the nation of Israel to their land before it ever happened. He foretold the end from the beginning over two thousand years in advance and then made it come to pass.

Only God could have done that. And since almighty God, Creator of the universe, is the One doing it, it's pointless to try to stop Him or interfere with the process.

God says in Jeremiah 32 that His heart is set on bringing the Jews back to their land and restoring them unto Himself.

I will surely gather them from all the lands where I banishthem in my furious anger and great wrath; I will bring themback to this place and let them live in safety.

They will be my people, and I will be their God.

I will give them singleness of heart and action, so that they will always fear me for their own good and the good of their children after them.

I will make an everlasting covenant with them: I will never stop doing good to them, and I will inspire them to fear me, so that they will never turn away from me.

I will rejoice in doing them good and will assuredly plant them in this land with all my heart and soul.

Jeremiah 32:37-41 NIV

When God says He is going to do something with all His heart and soul, our ears ought to perk up, and two things ought to come to mind: (1) stay out of the way, and (2) get with the program.

Hook up with His plan. Follow His lead. That would be the intelligent thing to do.

Yet the nations of the world, under the inspiration of the devil, have insisted on going their own willful way, and have set themselves in opposition to the plan of God.

What a bad idea.

In fact, the Bible makes it plain that by opposing God, these nations are bringing certain judgment upon themselves. Let's look at some verses that discuss this.

'In those days and at that time, when I restore the fortunes of Judah and Jerusalem,

I will gather all nations and bring them down to the Valley of Jehoshaphat. There I will enter into judgment against them concerning my inheritance, my people Israel, for they scattered my people among the nations and *divided up my land.'*[2]

Joel 3:1,2 NIV

But now many nations are gathered against you. They say, "Let her be defiled, let our eyes gloat over Zion!"

But they do not know the thoughts of the Lord; they do not understand his plan, he who gathers them like sheaves to the threshing floor.

"Rise and thresh, O Daughter of Zion, for I will give you horns of iron; I will give you hoofs of bronze and you will break to pieces many nations." You will devote their ill-gotten gains to the Lord, their wealth to the Lord of all the earth.

Micah 4:11-13 NIV

As in the days of your coming forth from the land of Egypt, I will show them marvelous things.

The nations shall see [God's deliverance] and be ashamed of all their might [which cannot be compared to His]. They shall lay their hands upon their mouths in consternation; their ears shall be deaf.

They shall lick the dust like a serpent; like crawling things of the earth they shall come trembling out of their strongholds and close places. They shall turn and come with fear and dread to the Lord our God and shall be afraid and stand in awe because of You [O Lord].

Micah 7:15-17 AMP

Perhaps the best-known biblical illustration of the nations bringing judgment upon themselves is the story of the Exodus. Thanks to Hollywood and the wonders of satellite television, this tremendous story is probably well-known throughout much of the world. The bottom line is that God absolutely humiliated the gods of Egypt, the world empire at that time, and delivered His people in a mighty way.

I believe that we're about to witness a sequel—only on a global scale.

Because so many of the peoples of the earth have turned their backs on the Word of God, they have fallen into deception and have become enslaved to false religions and false gods, just as Paul said they would.

> See to it that no one carries you off as spoil or makes you yourselves captive by his so-called philosophy and intellectualism and vain deceit (idle fancies and plain nonsense), following human tradition (men's ideas of the material rather than the spiritual world), just crude notions following the rudimentary and elemental teachings of the universe and disregarding [the teachings of] Christ (the Messiah).
>
> Colossians 2:8 AMP

Unfortunately, over the years some well-meaning (and some not-so-well-meaning) individuals have been complicit in this deception by encouraging people to believe the lie that we all ought to worship whatever god suits us best.

The remedy for darkness, however, is light, not lies.

Certainly we are not suggesting that we do away with the freedom of religion. God Himself does not *force* people to worship Him, and neither should we.

But that doesn't mean He condones the matter, either.

I'm sure you're familiar with the first of the Ten Commandments, found in Exodus 20:3, "Thou shalt have no other gods before me."

That's pretty straightforward, but the statement seems even stronger in the Hebrew translation.

> You shall not recognize the gods of others in My presence.
>
> Exodus 20:3 (The Tanach)[3]

Rabbinical commentary on this passage states that the phrase "in My presence" actually means "as long as I exist."[4] Considering that God exists in all places at all times, that doesn't really leave a lot of room for exceptions.

This would be a good thing for world leaders to keep in mind. Politically correct polytheism may be the world's "mantra" of the day, but it's repulsive to God. And His is the only opinion that really matters. If they want to see His blessings on their nation, they're going to have to be more concerned about pleasing Him than pleasing people.

THE COMING SHOWDOWN

What's been going on in the Middle East and what's been happening in the rest of the world since 9-11 is not really about nation against nation. It's not about land or the clash of civilizations. It's the ultimate "Battle of the Gods," as Osama Bin Laden alluded to just weeks after 9-11. On October 10, 2001, a spokesman for him made this statement on his behalf:

> *Jihad today is a religious duty of every Muslim. …God says fight, for the sake of God and to uphold the name of God…. Every Muslim has to play his real and true role to uphold his religion and his nation in fighting, and jihad is a duty…. This battle is a decisive battle between faithlessness and faith.*[5]

In Jerusalem, the Muslim Dome of the Rock now stands on the very site where the previous two Jewish temples stood. Although the exterior of the Dome has become instantly recognizable because of its notoriety in the news, not many people are aware of its interior.

Albert Hourani in *A History of the Arab Peoples* shares this fascinating insight about it:

> *The building of the Dome in this place has been convincingly interpreted as a symbolic act placing Islam in the lineage of Abraham and dissociating it from Judaism and Christianity. The inscriptions around the interior, the earliest known physical embodiment of texts from the Qur'an, proclaim the greatness of God, "the Mighty, the Wise," declare that "God and His angels bless the Prophet," and call upon Christians to*

recognize Jesus as an apostle of God, His word and spirit, but not His son.[6]

I believe that for nearly 1,300 years, that blasphemy has stood there as a fulfillment of Ezekiel 36:2, which says that the enemy has said of Israel, "...Aha, even the ancient high places are ours in possession."

Think about it. On the very place where the Most High God chose to put His Name and His Presence in the earth, the devil has built a house of worship for himself. You can almost hear him shouting, *"Mine!"*

But many believe that God's about to set the record straight, that we're about to see His glory manifested in the earth like we've never seen it before. The Bible's description of this sounds as if it's going to be a show-down that will make the Exodus and Elijah's triumph over the prophets of Baal on Mount Carmel look like child's play.[7]

Ezekiel 35 is a prophecy against the enemies of Israel. In it, God makes it clear that there will be a day when He wipes away the confusion about who the real God is.

The word of the Lord came to me:

"Son of man, set your face against Mount Seir; prophesy against it

and say: 'This is what the Sovereign Lord says: I am against you, Mount Seir, and I will stretch out my hand against you and make you a desolate waste.

I will turn your towns into ruins and you will be desolate. Then you will know that I am the Lord.

"'Because you harbored an ancient hostility and delivered the Israelites over to the sword at the time of their calamity, the time their punishment reached its climax,

therefore as surely as I live, declares the Sovereign Lord, I will give you over to bloodshed and it will pursue you. Since you did not hate bloodshed, bloodshed will pursue you.

I will make Mount Seir a desolate waste and cut off from it all who come and go.

I will fill your mountains with the slain; those killed by the sword will fall on your hills and in your valleys and in all your ravines.

I will make you desolate forever; your towns will not be inhabited. Then you will know that I am the Lord.

"'Because you have said, "These two nations and countries [Israel and Judah] will be ours and we will take possession of them," even though I the Lord was there, therefore as surely as I live, declares the Sovereign Lord, I will treat you in accordance with the anger and jealousy you showed in your hatred of them and I will make myself known among them when I judge you.

Then you will know that I the Lord have heard all the contemptible things you have said against the mountains of Israel [part of the area known today as the West Bank]. You said, "They have been laid waste and have been given over to us to devour."

You boasted against me and spoke against me without restraint, and I heard it.

This is what the Sovereign Lord says: While the whole earth rejoices, I will make you desolate.

Because you rejoiced when the inheritance of the house of Israel became desolate, that is how I will treat you. You will be desolate, O Mount Seir, you and all of Edom. Then they will know that I am the Lord.'"

Ezekiel 35:1-15 NIV

Four times in this brief chapter we see the expression "they will know that *I* am the Lord"—not Allah, not Muhammad, not Buddha, not Krishna or anybody else you might want to name, but Yahweh, King of the universe, the God of Abraham, Isaac, and Jacob.

We must not forget that the central issue here is the Person and plan of God. These nations are not coming under judgment just because they're opposing Israel (although Genesis 12:3 seems to support that fact) or because they're opposing the United States. These nations are coming under judgment because they're opposing God.

God has made some promises regarding Israel. If He *won't* keep them, He's a liar. If He *can't* keep them, He's an imposter. Either way, the devil wins.

Obviously, as we see throughout the Scriptures, that's not going to happen. But the devil's giving it his best shot. And that's really what all of this is about. The devil wants to be God. He has for a long, long time—and he's still working on it.

Along the way, he's deceived a lot of people into thinking he's right. He's manipulated them and exploited them and caused them to live on a level far below the life they were born to live.

God didn't create us to become the playthings of the devil. Jeremiah 29:11 tells us that God has plans to prosper us and to give us a hope and a future.

His preference is that people learn that truth by revelation (from the Word or by receiving revelation knowledge in our inner man, revealed to us by the Holy Spirit). Unfortunately, some people's hearts have become so hard that they won't see it until God's judgment is in the earth.

> ...for [only] when Your judgments are in the earth will the inhabitants of the world learn righteousness (uprightness and right standing with God).
>
> Though favor is shown to the wicked, yet they do not learn righteousness; in the land of uprightness they deal perversely and refuse to see the majesty of the Lord.
>
> Isaiah 26:9,10 AMP

Up until now, the nations may not have realized that they've been fighting against the One True God. But everything that's been happening in the world points to the fact that they're about to find out.

MAINTAIN PERSPECTIVE

The Church should respond to all this with compassion.

This is the time for us as believers to rise up and be loving teachers and examples of truth that will cause others to draw near to God. One way we can start is by practicing the principles discussed in this book. And above all, we need to be praying that people's eyes will be opened to the truth so that they will repent and turn to God before it's too late. He is merciful and will hear the cries of those who call on His Name with a humble heart.

It's also very important that we don't lose our perspective. No matter how bad things may look at times, we have to remember that things are ultimately going to go God's way, and we need to stay focused on Him (by reading the Word and talking to Him daily) if we want to live in victory.

In his book *Grant Takes Command,* author Bruce Catton makes a revealing observation about events near the end of the Civil War.

> *...The key to everything was the point Grant had made in his midwinter dispatch to Halleck—that "the enemy have not got army enough" to resist the pressure that would be exerted if all the major Union armies moved in proper coordination. The government had the strength to win if it applied it properly. It was up to Grant to apply it.*[8]

As we know, Grant *did* apply that strength. The rest is history.

Spiritually, we find ourselves in a similar situation. The difference in our case is that the war is already over, as we read earlier in Colossians 2:15. God has already defeated the enemy. Our mission now is to continually enforce that defeat and declare God's victory throughout the earth.

Unfortunately, we haven't always done a very good job of that. We've fallen for the lies of the devil and let ourselves be intimidated. We've cowered in the corners of life instead of boldly possessing the land God said was ours.

How did that happen?

We lost our perspective. We looked at things with natural eyes instead of spiritual ones. We focused on the temporal instead of the eternal.

The Bible tells the story of a man named Gehazi who had the same problem. Although Gehazi was the servant of the prophet Elisha and had witnessed many miraculous things as a result of being in that position, he panicked when he saw the enemy (the Syrian army) surrounding them.

> Then [the king] sent horses and chariots and a strong force there. They went by night and surrounded the city.

When the servant of the man of God got up and went out early the next morning, an army with horses and chariots had surrounded the city. "Oh, my lord, what shall we do?" the servant asked.

"Don't be afraid," the prophet answered. "Those who are with us are more than those who are with them."

And Elisha prayed, "O Lord, open his eyes so he may see." Then the Lord opened the servant's eyes, and he looked and saw the hills full of horses and chariots of fire all around Elisha.

2 Kings 6:14–17 NIV

Notice that Gehazi panicked, but Elisha never batted an eye. He knew his God, and he knew his place in God. As a result, nothing the enemy did fazed him.

Perception is everything. Correct perception was the key to Elisha's victory. Correct perception was the key to Grant's victory. Correct perception is the key to our victory.

The days of any part of the Church being weak and beaten-down are over. God is sending out a fresh call into the hearts of His people to rise up and walk in the fullness of the victory He has provided for us—not just for our sake, but for the sake of the harvest, for the sake of people's eternal destinies.

But that's going to require maintaining the correct perspective on our part. We're going to have to know our God, and we're going to have to know who we are in Him.[9]

Once we do, and once we start walking in the reality of those truths, the threats of the enemy won't faze us. After all, he simply doesn't have "army enough," and there's ultimately nothing he can do to stop us.

ENDNOTES

Preface

[1] The term "last days" is mentioned frequently in the Bible, including in Genesis 49:1, Acts 2:17, 2 Timothy 3:1, and 2 Peter 3:3. It refers to "...the close of the existing, and beginning of the final, dispensation; of which Christ's second coming shall be the consummation." *Jamieson, Fausset and Brown Commentary* (Electronic Database: Biblesoft, 1997), s.v. "Hebrews 1:2." All rights reserved.

Introduction

[1] *Merriam-Webster OnLine Dictionary,* copyright © 2002, s.v. "army," available from <http://www.m-w.com>.

[2] W.E. Vine, *An Expository Dictionary of New Testament Words* (Old Tappan, New Jersey: Fleming H. Revell Company, 1966), p. 311, s.v. "SABAOTH."

[3] Francis Trevelyan Miller, *History of World War II* (Iowa Falls, Iowa: Riverside Book and Bible House, 1945), p. 230.

Principle #1

[1] Russell F. Weigley, *History of the United States Army* (Bloomington: Indiana University Press, 1984), p. 252.

[2] Bruce Catton, *Reflections on the Civil War* (Garden City, NY: Doubleday & Co., Inc., 1981), p. 12.

[3] William Seymour, *Decisive Factors in Twenty Great Battles of the World* (New York: St. Martin's Press, 1988), p. 359.

[4] Holy or holiness is generally used to indicate sanctity or separation from anything that is sinful, impure, or morally imperfect. Based on information from *New Unger's Bible Dictionary* (originally published by Moody Press of Chicago, Illinois, 1988).

[5] "Holy" is part of God's nature; while He tells us to "Be holy" (1 Peter 1:16), we can never attain holiness through our own efforts, but only by the power of the Holy Spirit in us. We receive the Holy Spirit when we ask Jesus into our heart; we receive the fullness of the Holy Spirit in the same way, by asking God to fill us with His Spirit.

Principle #2

[1] David Nevin, *Sherman's March: Atlanta to the Sea* (Alexandria, Virginia: Time-Life Books, Inc., 1986), p. 127.

[2] William Seymour, p. 224.

[3] North Callahan, *George Washington: Soldier and Man* (New York: William Morrow & Co., Inc., 1972), p. 99.

[4] James E. Strong, "Greek Dictionary of the New Testament" in *Strong's Exhaustive Concordance of the Bible* (Nashville: Abingdon, 1890), p. 47, entry #3306, s.v. "abide," John 15:7.

[5] Based on a definition from Vine, p. 196, s.v. "CLEAVE, CLAVE, 1. KOLLAO."

[6] Yitzhak Buxbaum, *Jewish Spiritual Practices* (Northvale, New Jersey: Jason Aronson, Inc., 1990), p. 3.

[7] Ibid.

[8] J. Oswald Sanders, *Enjoying Intimacy With God* (Chicago: Moody Press, 1980), p. 12.

[9] Oswald Chambers, *My Utmost For His Highest* (New York: Dodd, Mead & Company, 1935), p. 72, s.v. "March 12, ABANDONMENT."

[10] Merriam-Webster, s.v. "abandon."

[11] Ibid, s.v. "wonderful."

[12] Based on a definition from Merriam-Webster, s.v. "marvelous."

[13] Ibid, s.v. "rebellion."

[14] *Webster's Ninth New Collegiate Dictionary* (Springfield, Massachusetts: Merriam-Webster Inc., Publishers, 1985), s.v. "woe."

Principle #3

[1] Martin Ebon, *The Soviet Propaganda Machine* (New York: McGraw-Hill Book Co., 1987), p. 401.

[2] Francis Trevelyan Miller, p. 894.

[3] Charles Grant, *Wargame Tactics* (New York: Hippocrene Books, Inc., 1979), p. 3.

[4] Francis Trevelyan Miller, p. 63.

[5] C.S. Lewis, *The Screwtape Letters* (New York: The Macmillan Company, 1961), p. 9.

[6] Ibid., p. iii.

[7] Merriam-Webster, s.v. "omni-."

[8] Based on definitions from Merriam-Webster, s.v. "omnipotent"; "omnipresent"; "omniscient."

[9] "Some have given another sense of this, as looking back to the fall of the angels, and designed for a caution to these disciples, lest their success should puff them up with pride...that was the sin for which Satan was *cast down from heaven,* where he had been an angel of light I saw it, and give you an intimation of it." *Matthew Henry Complete Commentary on the Whole Bible,*

"Commentary on Luke 10," available from <http://bible.cross-walk.com/Commentaries/MatthewHenryComplete/mhc-com.cgi?book=lu&chapter=010>; 1706.

[10] Merriam-Webster, s.v. "fling."

[11] Ibid, s.v. "may."

[12] Ibid, s.v. "curse."

[13] Ibid, s.v. "deceive."

[14] Ibid, s.v. "oppress."

[15] Ibid, s.v. "fraud."

[16] Ibid, s.v. "disinformation."

[17] Based on information from Albert Barnes, D.D., *Barnes' Notes* (Electronic Database: Biblesoft, 1997), s.v. "James 4:7." All rights reserved.

[18] Ibid, s.v. "flee."

[19] Merriam-Webster, s.v. "noise."

[20] "The Christian life is often represented as a journey, and the word walk, in the Scripture, is often equivalent to live...[In the Spirit] Live under the influences of the Holy Spirit; admit those influences fully into your hearts." *Barnes' Notes,* s.v. "Galatians 5:16."

[21] Merriam-Webster, s.v. "wield."

Principle #4

[1] Francis Trevelyan Miller, p. 416.

[2] Ibid., pp. 708,709.

[3] Ibid., p. 601.

[4] Charles Grant, p. 113.

[5] Merriam-Webster, s.v. "bent."

Principle #5

[1] Burke Davis, *George Washington and the American Revolution* (New York: Random House, Inc., 1975), pp. 118,119.

[2] Ibid, p. 353.

[3] Bruce Catton, *Grant Takes Command* (Boston: Little, Brown and Company, Inc., 1968), p. 335.

[4] "...it was a mistaken patriotism, which idolized the well being of his [Jonah's] own and God's people, and desired that its enemy, the appointed instrument of its chastisement, should be itself destroyed." *Barnes' Notes,* s.v. "Jonah 4:1."

[5] "The anointing with oil was a symbol of endowment with the Spirit of God...for the duties of the office to which a person was consecrated." *New Unger's Bible Dictionary,* originally published by Moody Press of Chicago, Illinois, 1988. Used by permission.

[6] Merriam-Webster, s.v. "fiery."

Principle #6

[1] William Seymour, p. 243.

[2] Colonel Michael Dewar, *The Art of Deception in Warfare* (New York: Sterling Publishing Co., Inc., 1989), p. 13.

[3] Merriam-Webster, s.v. "obedient."

[4] Ibid, s.v. "presumptuous."

[5] Ibid, s.v. "presume."

[6] *Barnes' Notes,* s.v. "Psalm 19:13."

Conclusion

[1] Isaiah 14:12-17; Revelation 20:1-3.

[2] Since it is not within the scope of this text to cover in detail the issue of Israel's right to the land, a recommended reading list on this subject has been included at the end of this book.

[3] *The Artscroll Series/Stone Edition, The Tanach, Student Size Edition* (Brooklyn, New York: Mesorah Publications, Ltd. 1996, 1998), p. 183, s.v. "Exodus 20:3."

[4] Rabbi Nosson Scherman, *The Chumash* (Brooklyn, New York: Mesorah Publications, 2000), p. 408.

[5] "Text of Al-Qaeda statement on U.S. attacks, presented by Sulaiman Abu Ghaith, a spokesman for Osama Bin Laden," *Financial Times,* October 10, 2001, available from <http://news.ft.com/home/us>.

[6] Albert Hourani, *A History of the Arab Peoples* (New York: MJF Books, 1991), p. 28.

[7] 1 Kings 18:19-40.

[8] Bruce Catton, p. 167.

[9] Romans 8:17; 2 Corinthians 5:17.

REFERENCES

Buxbaum, Yitzhak. *Jewish Spiritual Practices*. Northvale, New Jersey: Jason Aronson, Inc., 1990.

Callahan, North. *George Washington: Soldier and Man*. New York: William Morrow & Co., Inc., 1972.

Catton, Bruce. *Grant Takes Command*. Boston: Little, Brown and Company, Inc., 1968, 1969.

Catton, Bruce. *Reflections on the Civil War*. Garden City, New York: Doubleday & Co., Inc., 1981.

Chambers, Oswald. *My Utmost for His Highest*. New York: Dodd, Mead & Company, 1935.

Davis, Burke. *George Washington and the American Revolution*. New York: Random House, Inc., 1975.

Dewar, Colonel Michael. *The Art of Deception in Warfare*. New York: Sterling Publishing Co., Inc., 1989.

Ebon, Martin. *The Soviet Propaganda Machine*. New York: McGraw-Hill Book Co., 1987.

Grant, Charles. *Wargame Tactics*. New York: Hippocrene Books, Inc., 1979.

Lewis, C.S. *The Screwtape Letters*. New York: The Macmillan Company, 1961.

Miller, Francis Trevelyan. *History of World War II*. Iowa Falls, Iowa: Riverside Book and Bible House, 1945.

Nevin, David. *Sherman's March: Atlanta to the Sea*. Alexandria, Virginia: Time-Life Books, Inc., 1986.

Sanders, J. Oswald. *Enjoying Intimacy With God*. Chicago: Moody Press, 1980.

Seymour, William. *Decisive Factors in Twenty Great Battles of the World*. New York: St. Martin's Press, 1988.

Weigley, Russell F. *History of the United States Army*. Bloomington: Indiana University Press, 1984.

Recommended Reading on Israel's Land Rights

Archbold, Norma Parrish. *The Mountains of Israel.* Jerusalem: Phoebe's Song, 2001.

Peters, Joan. *From Time Immemorial.* Chicago: JKAP Publishing, 1984.

PRAYER OF SALVATION

God loves you—no matter who you are, no matter what your past. God loves you so much that He gave His one and only begotten Son for you. The Bible tells us that "...whoever believes in him shall not perish but have eternal life" (John 3:16 NIV). Jesus laid down His life and rose again so that we could spend eternity with Him in heaven and experience His absolute best on earth. If you would like to receive Jesus into your life, say the following prayer out loud and mean it from your heart.

Heavenly Father, I come to You admitting that I am a sinner. Right now, I choose to turn away from sin, and I ask You to cleanse me of all unrighteousness. I believe that Your Son, Jesus, died on the cross to take away my sins. I also believe that He rose again from the dead so that I might be forgiven of my sins and made righteous through faith in Him. I call upon the name of Jesus Christ to be the Savior and Lord of my life. Jesus, I choose to follow You and ask that You fill me with the power of the Holy Spirit. I declare that right now I am a child of God. I am free from sin and full of the righteousness of God. I am saved in Jesus' name. Amen.

If you prayed this prayer to receive Jesus Christ as your Savior for the first time, please contact us on the web at www.harrisonhouse.com to receive a free book.

Or you may write to us at

Harrison House
P.O. Box 35035
Tulsa, Oklahoma 74153

ABOUT THE AUTHOR

Kim Freeman is a writer, researcher, and Bible teacher, whose practical, no-nonsense approach to the Word of God makes it both easy to understand and apply.

Born and raised in St. Louis, Missouri, Kim holds a bachelor of arts degree in psychology from the University of Missouri. Since 1987, she has served in various capacities on different church and ministry staffs and has a deep desire to see believers walk in the maturity of their faith.

Kim also possesses a tremendous love for Israel and the Jewish people, which has taken her to the Holy Land on several occasions, both for study and to offer practical assistance as a volunteer.

Currently serving as part of the management team at Church On The Rock in St. Peters, Missouri, she writes and teaches in the local church on a variety of topics related to spiritual growth and development. She also directs a church-based ministry designed to familiarize Christians with the Hebrew roots of Christianity, inform Christians of significant current events in Israel and the other prophetic nations, and show love and support to the Jewish community through various practical outreach projects and trips, both locally and in Israel.

To contact Kim Freeman
write:

P.O. Box 1668
St. Peters, MO 63376
(636) 240-7775
kfreeman@cotr.org

*Please include your prayer requests
and comments when you write.*

Additional copies of this book
are available from your local bookstore.

If this book has been a blessing to you
or if you would like to see more of
the Harrison House product line,
please visit us on our Web site at
www.harrisonhouse.com

HARRISON HOUSE
Tulsa, Oklahoma 74153

THE HARRISON HOUSE VISION

Proclaiming the truth and the power

Of the Gospel of Jesus Christ

With excellence;

Challenging Christians to

Live victoriously,

Grow spiritually,

Know God intimately.